Friends, Faith and Feasts

Friends, Faith and Feasts

A Cookery Book
for Christian Festivals
and Saints' Days

Sylvia Hart

Copyright © Sylvia Hart 2006

British Library Cataloguing in Publication data
A catalogue record for this book is available
from the British Library

ISBN 1 85852 291 9

First published by Inspire
4 John Wesley Road
Werrington
Peterborough PE4 6ZP

Printed and bound in Great Britain by
Arrowsmith Printers, Bristol

Acknowledgements

Thanks to my husband Peter, for sharing his office with me; to my son and daughter-in-law John and Angela, for encouraging me to 'go for it' and get my manuscript published; to my son Ian, for sorting out my several computing problems, and to my sister Patricia, for letting me raid her bookshelves during my research and for answering my cookery queries.

Thanks also to Susan Hibbins, Assistant Editor at Inspire, who has worked hard to get the manuscript ready for publication, and to Lorna Valentine, who has designed the pages and brought her artistic talents to enhance the look of the book.

I acknowledge the help of all these people, and thank them sincerely for it.

Sylvia Hart

Contents

Introduction

In recent years there has been a resurgence of interest in the saints and in their example of lives devoted to God and to God's teaching. Saints are seen no longer as people with whom we have nothing in common; we can learn much from them, and from the way in which they tried to follow God's teaching.

Before the Reformation, saints' feast days were a reason for celebration, providing a lightening of the daily grind at a time when holidays were unknown. Often such celebrations included local fairs, at which merchants could sell their wares and men could sell their labour. Special food was part of the celebrations, and traditional recipes are still associated with saints' days. Customs and traditions are also linked to the major festivals of the Church year, and again, food was an important feature of them. Fish played a large part in diets which included several meat-free days a week and a strict observation of Lent.

Recipes varied in different parts of the country. In this book I have tried to track down some of these recipes, and to suggest modern alternatives and supplementary choices, including vegetarian options. Recipes are included for seasons of the Church year and for saints' days – it would be good to see a revival in celebrating together with special food as people did years ago.

A few of the recipes suggest the use of cider or ale, once widely used as everyday drinks. If you wish to make non-alcoholic versions, a good apple juice is a substitute for cider, and a good stock for ale.

Sylvia Hart
January 2006

Food in Britain

The diet of the average Iron Age Briton was a varied one, especially in wetland areas such as the East Anglian Fens and the Somerset Levels, where fish and fowl provided an abundance of food. Evidence has also been found of large numbers of domesticated livestock, such as sheep and goats, as well as wild pigs and 'aurochs' (huge wild cows standing six feet high at the shoulder), which would have provided plenty of meat for the population of the time. Feasting seems to have been an integral part of 'Celtic' Iron Age life – the idea that the wealthy always ate better than the poor was not necessarily correct.

The Roman invasion in AD 43 introduced animals, plants and fruits to Britain designed to make Roman life in this cold outpost of the Empire as comfortable as possible. Guinea fowl and pheasant were introduced by the Romans, and they also brought fruits with them, including cherries, to enliven their daily meals. Many varieties of fruit and vegetables already existed in pre-Roman Britain. Carrots were small and white, and apples small and bitter! The Romans introduced hybrids by crossing them with Mediterranean species, producing the varieties we recognize today.

Herbs, such as thyme, bay leaf, coriander and savoury mint and various spices were used, sometimes to disguise the taste of the food, especially meat, which was often bad. The Romans also imported garum fish oil, used throughout Europe to cover up the taste of fish that was not fresh, and olives, dates, wine and oil. Once Roman society was established in Britain, the food eaten in a wealthy villa would have been plentiful and varied, with fresh meat, bread, cheese, vegetables and fruit.

The Angles, Saxons and Jutes who settled successively in Britain brought with them some of their own traditional food and drink, but the basic diet of most people remained the same. Wheat, barley, rye and oats were grown; animals – cows, sheep, goats and pigs – were kept. Herbs and spices, some imported, like pepper, ginger, cinnamon and nutmeg, were used widely to flavour food, but we do not know exactly how, as the first recipe books were not produced until the fourteenth century. In the medieval period the wealthy ate capons, geese, larks and chicken, with fresh bread made from milled flour; the poorer people ate bread made from barley and rye, and potage made from onions, cabbage, garlic, leeks, nuts and anything else in season.

Fish and shellfish were important foods from Roman times. Fish that we might not consider, such as perch, pike and roach, were eaten as well as salmon, haddock, mackerel, trout, oysters, mussels, cockles and eels. When the Church decreed that people should eat fish several days a week, however, this usually meant, for most people, salted and pickled herrings. During Lent further restrictions were imposed on eggs and dairy products; and in monasteries fish was important since monks ate no meat at this time, a rule that was relaxed by the fifteenth century. During the summer months large numbers of herrings were salted to preserve them for transporting inland.

Salt was important for both flavouring and preserving from Roman times, and many salt pans have been found around the coasts of Britain. To improve the taste of food cooks used spice mixes – 'powder fort', which included ginger, pepper, mace and sometimes dried chives, and 'powder douce', containing ginger or cinnamon, nutmeg and sometimes cloves and a little pepper. The mixtures were much cheaper to buy than each component spice, as imported spices were very expensive.

Sugar as we buy it today was unknown in Britain until the 1100s, when it was brought into the country by the Crusaders. Before that large amounts of honey were used to sweeten food, and also in the brewing of mead. During the sixteenth century more sources of sugar became available, and in the 1540s a refinery was set up in London to produce white crystalline cones of sugar weighing almost 6.5 kilos. These were used in both savoury and sweet dishes. The annual consumption of sugar increased, the bulk of it eaten by the wealthy. The Elizabethans ate so much sugar that they were noted for their black teeth.

As well as being highly spiced, medieval food was colourful and scented. Rice puddings were coloured, custards were often red, and even meat balls were sometimes coated in gold leaf. Saffron was used for yellow colouring, sandalwood for red, parsley juice for green, and turnsole, or heliotropium, for purple. Although there was a wide variety of herbs and spices available for cooking, there was only one raising agent for many years – yeast – which is why many recipes in this book use yeast rather than baking powder.

Salads were eaten in medieval and Elizabethan times, and they too included herbs. Flowers were also added, such as primroses, violets and borage. Today we are rediscovering natural flavours like these from plants in our local environments. We might be surprised to learn that the medieval housewife dressed her salad with oil and vinegar, just as we do today. She was also conscious of the free food growing around her and, for example, used cob nuts instead of expensive almonds.

Fresh fruit has always been available in Britain, though how much was consumed by the resident population is not known. Berries formed part of people's diets from the very earliest times. The monasteries were a good source of fruit, since they set aside large areas for growing it, and for apple orchards (a good proportion of the fruit was used for making cider).

Kitchen equipment at the time was sparse and primitive; for example, when flour needed separating from bran it was sifted through a piece of coarse cloth such as canvas or linen. The flour that fell through was swept up with a small broom or goose wing. Knives, spoons and ladles were the main items of cutlery. The Romans had used forks for serving purposes, but they were not used by individuals to eat until the eighteenth century. For many years a kitchen's source of heat was a fire in the middle of the room, until it was moved to the side and was then able to incorporate an oven. Most food was cooked in a cauldron or baked in the embers of a fire wrapped in leaves or clay. Meat was also roasted on a large rotary spit or by using smaller skewers.

Most working families kept a pig or two; when they were slaughtered nearly all the animal could be eaten. (It is said that the only thing you cannot eat is the pig's squeak.) Sometimes farm labourers also kept a cow. Wealthy landowners kept cattle, sheep and goats for meat and for milk, and the milk was used for cream, cheese and butter. Poorer people used skimmed milk to make cheese so hard that it had to be soaked and beaten before it could be eaten.

Cookery notes

Yeast – as so many of the recipes in this book use yeast it is useful to find a source of fresh yeast. Bakers who bake on the premises may be able to help you and some delicatessens and health food shops also stock it. Some of the yeast recipes use vitamin C tablets, but this quick method can be used for all yeast recipes. This method cuts out the initial proving of the dough, so as soon as the dough is made it can be shaped and divided, and then covered and allowed to rise to double its size just once.

To test a large cake to see if it is cooked – push a fine knitting needle or skewer into the centre of the cake. If it comes out clean then the cake is cooked.

To prevent a cake from becoming too brown on top – cover the cake with a piece of brown paper or baking paper. The cake will continue to cook but the top will not burn. The problem arises because the cooking temperature is too high.

Temperature and timing – the make and age of a cooker will affect the temperature and timing for cooking, so those given in the recipes are only advisory. You may need to adjust them as necessary for your cooker.

To test if bread and rolls are cooked – tap the loaf or roll on the bottom and if it sounds hollow then the bread is cooked.

Cooking biscuits – the temperatures given in the recipes are high. If preferred, cook the biscuits at a lower temperature for a longer time. Slower cooking will mean you have longer to decide that the biscuits are cooked and they will be crisp when eaten.

To keep biscuits crisp – a few lumps of sugar put in with the biscuits in an air-tight container dries the air and keeps the biscuits crisp and fresh.

Cutters – it can be hard to find specially shaped cutters for mince pies and biscuits. It is easy enough to buy star, holly leaves, Christmas trees, men shapes etc. but more difficult if you want oval cutters or angel cutters. They are available, for example, from Divertimenti shops, or see their website www.divertimenti.co.uk.

Vanilla – vanilla pods are useful for flavouring milk and other liquids and their seeds add to the flavour. Sugar can be flavoured by storing it with vanilla pods. Never use vanilla flavouring, but always buy vanilla essence. The pods and the essence can seem expensive but they are well worth it.

Removing skins – quite often you need to remove the skins of tomatoes, nuts and, less frequently, Jerusalem artichokes. This can be done by first blanching them for a couple of minutes in boiling water and then putting them in cold water; the skins should then rub or peel off easily.

Seasoned flour – this is flour to which salt and pepper has been added to bring out the flavour of food which is coated in it.

5

Baking blind – pastry cases for flans and quiches are sometimes baked blind. This means that once the tin has been lined with pastry a piece of greaseproof paper or baking paper is put over the uncooked pastry in the bottom of the tin and special baking beans or haricot beans are put on the paper to stop the pastry bubbling. Once the pastry is nearly cooked the beans and paper are removed and the tin replaced in the oven for a couple of minutes to finish the cooking. The paper is there merely to ease the removal of the beans, but if no beans are available crumpled paper or foil can be used in their place.

Pastry – whilst a recipe for shortcrust pastry is given in the St Kentigern section (p. 97), perfectly good pastry can be bought frozen or chilled.

Bread – I have given some of the history of bread, bread-making and recipes for making bread slowly with fresh yeast and the faster method with fresh yeast and vitamin C, but very good bread can be made in bread-makers. There are also many flours available today, both in shops and by mail order.

Weights and measures – there is no precise correlation between imperial and metric measures and these will, therefore, vary a little from book to book. When making a recipe keep to either imperial or metric measurements.

Advent and Christmas

Although Advent is seen by many as the last four frantic weeks leading up to Christmas, in the Church it is a penitential season, during which time Christians prepare to welcome the Christ child once again into the world and into their hearts. Many of the traditions surrounding Advent and Christmas began as pagan rites in which people looked forward, when the winter was at its darkest, to the return of spring. The Advent wreath, for example, which is used in many churches today, originated in pre-Christian Germany when people made wreaths of evergreen and lit fires to remind themselves that winter would one day be over. Fire and light were important in the northern hemisphere when the days were short. As Christianity moved northwards it borrowed many pagan traditions; the fires of mid-winter became associated with the birth of Jesus, who brought light into a dark world.

Various dates have been suggested for the birth of Christ, which was not celebrated by the Church until the middle of the fourth century. In the Roman Empire 25 December was already a holiday, celebrating that the shortest day had passed and that the light would now increase. The first written reference was in a Roman document of AD 354, which mentioned 25 December as 'natus Christus in Betleem Iudeae'. Gradually the Church turned the pagan celebration into the religious festival of Christmas.

For many people Christmas dinner is the highlight of the celebrations, and roast turkey is still the traditional dish, though more people now choose other meats as well as vegetarian dishes. Until turkeys were available in Europe, people ate pork, goose and even peacock instead.

Although all the food that people like to eat at Christmas can now be bought at the supermarket, half the fun of Christmas is in the anticipation, cooking and making as many of the dishes as possible.

Roast turkey

Roast turkey is now the traditional main course, but previously it would have been roast goose or, for a smaller family, roast chicken. For stuffing and roasting a goose see the St Michael section (p. 134).

Cooking times

Weight of turkey	Time	Temperature
6-10lb/2.7-4.5kg	20 minutes per lb/450g plus 20 minutes	180°C/350°F/gas mark 4
10-18lb/4.5-8.1kg	15 minutes per lb/450g plus 15 minutes	180°C/350°F/gas mark 4

Turkey

The best bird is a female, 6-8 months old, weighing 10-12lbs/4.5-5.4kg. The only way you will know if it is male or female is to go to a turkey farm to choose a fresh bird. Fresh rather than frozen turkeys are more expensive but are worth the extra cost. Before cooking the bird lift the skin and spread a layer of butter between the skin and the flesh.

Arrange slices of streaky bacon on the breast of the turkey. They are a tasty addition to the meal, and also serve to moisten the meat which can be a little dry. It is best to wrap the turkey in foil for most of the cooking time, opening it just to brown the bird for the last 30 minutes.

Stuffings

These should be put in the neck cavity. If they are put in the body cavity it increases the cooking time, and sometimes the turkey is cooked and the stuffing is not.

Packet stuffings are perfectly acceptable, but can be greatly improved if you add more chestnuts (chopped), apricots (chopped) or cranberries – make your own variation to suit your taste.

One or two onions or a lemon can be put in the body cavity of the turkey to add flavour to the meat.

Sausage meat was once widely used as a stuffing, but it took a long time to cook and now chipolatas wrapped in streaky bacon are more commonly served as an accompaniment.

No Christmas dinner would be complete without roast potatoes and, among other vegetables, Brussels sprouts with chestnuts (usually twice as many sprouts as chestnuts, by weight). Cranberry sauce and bread sauce are also served with turkey.

Spiced beef

Ingredients

To serve about 6 people

4lb/2kg rolled salted
   silverside of beef
1 onion, peeled and sliced
1 small turnip, peeled and
   sliced
3 carrots, peeled and sliced
1 bay leaf
12 cloves
1 level tsp mustard
   powder
2oz/50g brown sugar
Juice of 1 lemon
$1/2$ tsp each ground
   cinnamon, allspice and
   nutmeg

Ingredients

1 pkt puff pastry
1 bag mixed vegetables or
   a selection of fresh
   vegetables chopped
   quite finely
1 tin condensed soup
   (celery is good); or a
   quantity of cheese
   sauce
1 tin or pack of whole or
   broken chestnuts
1 pkt frozen cranberries

This was traditionally eaten on Christmas Day and/or St Stephen's Day (26 December) and is a dish that can be served hot or cold. It should be brought to the table decorated with holly and red ribbons.

Method

Soak the meat in cold water overnight. The next day rinse it well and tie it up to form a neat joint. Put the onion, turnip and carrot in a large saucepan and place the meat on top of the vegetables, add the bay leaf and cover with cold water. Bring to the boil, skim off any fat and put the lid on the saucepan, reduce the heat and simmer gently for $3^1/_2$-4 hours. Leave the meat to cool completely in the liquid. Set the oven to 180°C/350°F/gas mark 4, drain the meat very thoroughly and put it in a roasting tin. Stick the cloves in the joint, then mix together the remaining ingredients and spread them over the beef. Bake the joint for 40 minutes, basting from time to time. Guinness can be added to the cooking liquid.

Vegetarian Christmas plait

This is a quick main course that can be made from ingredients that may well be in the cupboard and freezer, or can be made in advance and frozen until Christmas Eve. The size is adaptable too; it can be as large or small as is needed.

Method

Place a suitable amount of vegetables, pieces of chestnut and cranberries in a basin and blend together with sufficient soup or sauce. Roll out the pastry into a rectangle. Make slanting cuts on the pastry along the length of the two long sides.
Spoon the filling down the centre and fold the stips over this to make a plait. Brush the plait with milk or beaten egg and cook in a hot oven until it is golden brown. Serve with the usual Christmas vegetables.

Christmas pudding

Ingredients

To make 2 x 2 pint/1.2 litre puddings

4oz/100g plain flour
2 tsp mixed spice
$1/2$ tsp ground ginger
$1/2$ tsp ground nutmeg
4oz/100g fresh breadcrumbs
4oz/100g dark
    muscovado sugar
6oz/150g vegetable or
    beef suet
4oz/100g almonds,
    blanched and chopped
4oz/100g dried apricots,
    chopped
4oz/100g glacé cherries
2oz/50g candied peel,
    chopped
Grated rind of 1 lemon
Grated rind of 1 orange
8oz/225g cooking apples,
    grated
8oz/225g currants
10oz/275g raisins
12oz/350g sultanas
3 eggs, beaten
8fl oz/250ml brown ale
2 tbsp brandy or rum

There are a number of traditions associated with the Christmas pudding. All the family should take turns to stir the pudding mixture clockwise three times, and make a wish. In past years, when the mixture was put in the basin a clean, new silver coin was put in it. Whoever found the coin in their pudding on Christmas Day would have good luck in the coming year. Puddings should be made well in advance of Christmas. Traditionally they are made on the Sunday before Advent – 'Stir up Sunday', so-called because the Collect (special prayer) for that day begins, 'Stir up, O Lord, the wills of thy faithful people'. In modern services the phrase is now used in the Post Communion prayer.

Excellent puddings can be bought, but many families have a favourite recipe that has been handed down over the generations. The recipe below is a traditional one.

Traditional Christmas pudding
Method

Sift the flour and spices into a large mixing bowl, and stir in the breadcrumbs, sugar and suet. Add the almonds, apricots, cherries, candied peel, lemon and orange rind, apple and dried fruit and mix well. Add the eggs, ale and brandy or rum and mix well.
Line the base of two greased 2 pint/1.2 litre pudding basins with a circle of greaseproof paper or baking paper. Spoon the pudding mixture into the basins and smooth the tops. Cover each pudding with two rounds of greaseproof paper, pleated across the middle to allow for

expansion, and tie down with string. Put each pudding in a large saucepan and pour in enough boiling water to come halfway up the pudding basins. Bring to the boil, then reduce the heat and cover with a tight-fitting lid. Steam each pudding for 3 hours, topping up with boiling water as necessary to ensure the saucepans do not boil dry. Remove the basins from the saucepans and leave them to cool. Remove the paper and cover with fresh greaseproof paper tightly tied down. Store in a cool, dry place for up to 12 months. Steam for a further 3 hours before serving.

Slices of pudding can be frozen and can be gently reheated in a microwave – they do burn very quickly so take care in selecting the power and the time for this.

Ingredients

$^{1}/_{2}$ pint/250ml double cream
4 eggs, separated
4oz/100g icing sugar
1 level tsp mixed spice
4oz/100g mixed dried fruit
   soaked in brandy or rum
   overnight (it makes a more
   festive ice-cream if the fruit
   includes glazed pineapple,
   apricots and different
   coloured cherries as well as
   the raisins)

Ice-cream Christmas pudding

This is a simple ice-cream to which you can add the dried fruit and spices of the traditional Christmas pudding. It can be made well in advance and will keep for months in the freezer. Adding a teaspoonful of vanilla essence instead of the fruit and spice, it makes a useful addition to any dessert.

Method

In a large bowl whisk the egg whites until they are stiff. In a separate bowl whisk the cream until it is thick, but not lumpy. In a small basin beat the egg yolks, add 1oz of the icing sugar and beat it in. Add this egg yolk mixture to the cream and whisk well. Add the remaining sugar to the egg white and stir in more gently. Now add the cream mixture to the meringue and mix well, then stir in the spice and the drained fruit. Tip the mixture into a suitable container and put in the freezer until needed. Take the ice-cream out of the freezer a few minutes before serving to allow it to soften.

Mince pies

A wide range of mince pies is on offer in the shops, but it is fun to make your own. As it is Christmas why not try making a special pastry, such as Rose Pastry (see opposite)? If you don't have the time to make or the space to store your own mincemeat some 'luxury' versions are available, and you can always add extra fruit, especially chopped cherries, and a little 'spirit', if you wish.

These little pies, filled with spicy mincemeat, have been traditional Christmas fare for centuries. It was customary to eat one pie every day for the 12 days of Christmas to ensure 12 happy months ahead. Mince pies should be flat, not deep filled, and they should be oval to represent the shape of the crib. Oval cutters are available, they may take some finding, but they are stocked by specialist cooking/catering shops (see p. 5). The spices were said to represent the exotic gifts brought to the Christ child by the Magi.

Ingredients

To make 5¹/₂lb/2.5kg

3¹/₂lb/1.6kg mixed dried fruit
8oz/225g cooking apples,
    peeled, cored and grated
4oz/100g blanched almonds,
    chopped
1lb/450g dark, soft brown
    sugar
6oz/175g shredded vegetable
    or beef suet
1 tsp grated nutmeg
1 tsp ground cinnamon
Grated rind and juice of
    1 lemon
Grated rind and juice
    of 1 orange
¹/₂ pint/300ml sherry or brandy

Mincemeat

Originally this was a way of preserving meat for use through the winter months. It contained minced beef and/or tongue mixed with dried fruit, and was highly spiced, preserved by the addition of brandy or other spirits. Today, in place of the meat, suet and apples are added to the mixture. Mincemeat improves with keeping and should be made a couple of weeks before use. It will remain fresh for six months if it is stored in a container with a plastic or screw-on top to prevent it from drying out.

Method

Put the dried fruit, cooking apples and almonds in a large bowl. (It is best to use a hard, firm apple as a juicy one may make the mixture too moist.) Add the sugar, suet, spices, lemon and orange rind and juice and the brandy or sherry and mix all the ingredients together thoroughly. Cover the mincemeat and leave to stand for two days. Stir well, put into sterilized jars and cover. Leave for two weeks before using.

Rose pastry
Ingredients

1lb/450g plain flour
10oz/250g butter
2oz/50g caster sugar
1 egg

Method

Rub the butter into the flour, stir in the sugar and bind the pastry together with the egg.
Make the pastry into a ball and allow it to rest in the refrigerator for about 30 minutes before use.

Mince pies
Ingredients

Special or ordinary shortcrust pastry
Homemade or shop mincemeat
1 egg white
Caster sugar
    for sprinkling

Brandy Butter
Serve with Christmas pudding or warm mince pies. Blend together 4oz/100g unsalted butter with 2 tbsp caster sugar. When it is light and fluffy slowly add 4 tbsp of brandy, beating thoroughly between each addition.

Rum Butter
This was first made to be served with oatcakes at Christenings, but has extended its use to be served with Christmas pudding, Coventry Godcakes (see p. 15) and warm mince pies.

Blend together 8oz/225g unsalted butter with 4oz/100g light, soft brown sugar, then beat in $1/_2$ tsp freshly grated nutmeg and $1/_2$ tsp lemon juice. Slowly beat in 3-4 tbsp of rum, beating well between additions to prevent curdling.

Method

Cut out ovals of pastry 2$1/_2$in/7cm long. Place half of them on greased and floured or lined baking sheets, and put a good teaspoonful of mincemeat in the middle of each oval. Dampen the edges around the mincemeat with milk and place another 2$1/_2$in/7cm oval of pastry on top of the first, pressing the edges down to seal in the filling. Make a small slit in the top and brush with the egg white and sprinkle with caster sugar.
Bake in a pre-heated oven 220°C/425°F/gas mark 7 for about 20 minutes or until golden brown. Allow the pies to stand for about 3 minutes before lifting them onto a wire rack to complete cooling. Serve the pies with cream or brandy butter or rum butter.

The original mince pie

Ingredients

1¹/₂lb/625g lean mutton or
 beef, minced
4oz/100g suet
2oz/50g raisins
2oz/50g currants
2oz/50g stoned prunes,
 chopped
¹/₂ tsp ground cloves
1 tsp ground mace
¹/₂ tsp black pepper
A pinch of saffron

For the pastry

1lb/450g plain flour
2 tsp salt
4oz/100g lard
¹/₄ pint/150ml water
4 tsp milk

For the glaze

1 tsp each of butter, rosewater
 and sugar melted together

This pie combines meat, suet and dried fruit and may seem strange to us today, but it still makes an excellent different dish for the Christmas season. The pie is substantial and finely flavoured, being especially well suited to buffet meals.

Method

Mix together the meat, suet, dried fruit, spices, pepper and saffron.

To make the pastry, sift the flour and salt together into a large mixing bowl and make a well in the middle. Heat the lard, water and milk to boiling point and pour this into the well. Beat the mixture together with a spoon to form a soft dough and then knead the dough on a floured surface until it is smooth. Cut off a quarter of the pastry and keep it covered until it is needed for the lid. Mould the larger piece of pastry to cover the base and sides of a loose-bottomed cake tin 8in/20cm diameter and 2in/5cm deep.

Pack the meat mixture into the pie and dampen the top edges of the side wall pastry. Roll the remaining pastry out to form the lid, press this firmly in place using the dampened pastry to make a good seal. Trim off excess pastry and use this to make decorations for the top of the pie. Cut a hole in the centre of the lid. Bake in the middle of a preheated oven 220°C/425°F/gas mark 7 for 15 minutes, then reduce the heat to 180°C/350°F/gas mark 4 and bake for a further 1¹/₄ hours.

Remove from the oven and brush with the glaze, then return the pie to the oven for a futher 15 minutes. Serve cold.

God's ketchels

Ingredients

1lb/450g bought puff pastry
Caster sugar for sprinkling

For the filling

2oz/50g butter, melted
8oz/225g currants
3oz/75g candied peel,
   chopped
2oz/50g ground almonds
$\frac{1}{2}$ tsp ground cinnamon
1 tsp ground nutmeg

'Ask me a blessing and I will give you a ketchel' is an old country saying. Godparents gave these cakes to their godchildren if they visited during the 12 days of Christmas.

Method

Divide the pastry into two equal pieces and roll each piece out into a square. Moisten the edges of each piece with water.

Combine the filling ingredients and spread them evenly over one piece of pastry, to within $\frac{1}{2}$in/1cm of the edge. Cover with the second square of pastry and press the edges firmly together.

Now mark the top of the pastry into 2in/5cm squares, pressing down but being careful not to cut through the pastry. Bake in a pre-heated oven 200°C/400°F/gas mark 6 for about 25 minutes or until golden brown. Whilst still hot sprinkle the ketchel with caster sugar and divide it into the small cakes as marked.

Coventry Godcakes

Coventry Godcakes are a variation of God's Ketchels, made in homes and bakeries in Warwickshire. They are triangular and vary greatly in size. Fill with mincemeat and once baked brush with lightly beaten egg white, sprinkle sugar on the top and return to the oven for a couple of minutes. These cakes were given by godparents to their godchildren to bring them luck in the coming year.

Christmas cakes

Ingredients

12oz/350g currants
8oz/225g raisins
8oz/225g sultanas
3oz/75g candied peel,
    chopped
4oz/100g glacé cherries,
    halved
2oz/50g almonds, blanched
    and chopped
Rind and juice of 1 lemon
6 tbsp brandy
12oz/350g plain flour
1 tsp mixed spice
1 tsp ground cinnamon
$1/_2$ tsp freshly grated nutmeg
9oz/250g butter
9oz/250g dark muscovado
    sugar
4 eggs, beaten

There are many recipes for Christmas cakes and most families may have their own favourite. As tastes change the traditional cake is too rich for some people and included here is a recipe for a plainer celebration cake.

Traditional cake
Method

Grease and line a 8in/20cm round or 7in/18cm square deep cake tin.

In a bowl mix the dried fruit, candied peel, cherries and almonds together with the lemon rind and juice and 2 tablespoons of brandy. In a separate bowl sift the flour and spices. In a third large mixing bowl cream together the butter and sugar and beat until light and fluffy, then add the eggs a little at a time alternating with a little flour to prevent curdling.

Fold in the flour, then stir in the fruit and mix thoroughly before spooning the mixture into the prepared tin. Bake in a pre-heated oven 150°C/300°/gas mark 2 for $3^1/_2$-4 hours or until it is firm to the touch and a knitting needle or fine skewer comes out cleanly when it is inserted into the middle of the cake. If the cake seems to be browning too much before this, cover the surface with a piece of foil or paper.

Remove the cake from the oven and allow it to begin to cool in the tin, then remove it from the tin and peel off the paper. When the cake is cool prick the base with a fine skewer or knitting needle and spoon over the remaining brandy, leaving the cake upside down to allow the brandy to soak in.

Wrap the cake in a double layer of greaseproof paper and then in foil. Store in a cool, dry place and the cake will keep for 12 months. Decorate with marzipan and icing as desired.
A recipe for marzipan can be found on p. 112.

Ingredients

To make a 7in/18cm square or 8in/20cm round cake

4oz/100g glacé cherries
4oz/100g crystallized pineapple
12oz/350g golden sultanas
4oz/100g chopped walnuts
6oz/175g butter
6oz/175g caster sugar
4 eggs
9oz/250g self-raising flour
3 tbsp sherry or whisky

Golden Christmas cake

A lighter and delicious cake that can be decorated in the traditional way or with a collection of jewel-coloured, crystallized fruits.

Method

Wash the pineapple and glacé cherries thoroughly and dry well. Chop these and mix them together.
Cream the butter and sugar until light and fluffy, and beat in the eggs and flour alternately to prevent curdling.
Fold in any remaining flour with the sherry or whisky.
Stir in the fruit and nuts and mix gently but well.
Spoon the mixture into a greased and lined cake tin and bake for one hour in a pre-heated oven 170°C/325°F/gas mark 3. Then reduce the heat to 150°C/300°F/gas mark 2 for a further $1^1/_2$-2 hours or until the cake is firm to the touch and a skewer comes out cleanly when the middle of the cake is pierced. Cool the cake in the tin for about 30 minutes, then complete cooling it on a wire rack.

Welsh toffee

Ingredients

To make about 1¹/₂ lb/800g

4oz/100g unsalted butter
1lb/450g granulated sugar
2 tbsp warm water
2 tbsp white vinegar
4 tbsp golden syrup or 2 tbsp
   each of syrup and treacle

Toffee-making was at one time an essential part of the Christmas and New Year celebrations in North Wales. Families and friends would come together for supper and at the end of the meal they would gather round the fire, tell stories and make toffee.

Method

Melt the butter in a large saucepan, stir in the sugar and remove the pan from the heat. Add the water, vinegar and syrup (or syrup and treacle) and stir over a low heat until the sugar dissolves. Do not let the mixture boil at this time.

Now bring the mixture to boiling point and boil steadily for 15-20 minutes or until a little of the toffee dropped into a bowl of cold water will snap. If you have a special thermometer the temperature should be 152°C/305°F.

Pour the toffee into a well-buttered tin 11in/28cm by 7in/18cm. Leave the toffee to cool and as soon as it begins to set mark the toffee into squares.

When the toffee is quite cold break it into the squares, wrap them in cellophane and store in an airtight tin or jar.

Frumenty/ferminty/firmity

Ingredients and method

Mix a teacup of the prepared wheat with 2oz/50g raisins, 2oz/50g currants, 2oz/50g sugar and 2 eggs.

Boil 2 pints/1 litre of milk and pour this over the fruit mixture and stir. This can be flavoured with nutmeg or cinnamon and sweetened with honey instead of sugar.

Brandy is sometimes added to this dish which can be eaten hot or cold or used as a filling for pasties.

There are different spellings for this dish which was eaten during the 12 days of Christmas, and also at any other church-based celebration. Looking at the recipes it may be hard to see why it was so popular! It was basically a type of porridge with fruit and added spices. Apparently the success of the dish depends on how the wheat (or sometimes pearl barley) is prepared.

The wheat should be put in a pan or stone jar with a lid. It is covered by three times its volume with cold water, put in a hot oven and left there as the oven cools for 24 hours. It can be put in a saucepan and covered with hot water and left similarly for 24 hours. The aim is for the grains to swell and burst and be set in a jelly. If this has not happened after a day, the process can be speeded up by boiling for five minutes.

Hodgkin

Ingredients and method

Start your Hodgkin with 1lb/450g of clean, hulled strawberries in a large stone jar or Rumtopf. Cover with 8oz/225g granulated or caster sugar. Pour in enough brandy to cover the fruit and sugar. Cover the jar with a tight-fitting lid. Repeat as fruits come into season, adding 1lb/450g of fresh fruit, 8oz/225g sugar and brandy. Stir the contents gently with each addition.

This is a diminutive form of 'hodgepodge' and is a fifteenth-century term for a mixture. This came back into popularity in the 1980s when Rumtopfs became popular. A Hodgkin takes all summer to make as fruits are added from June to late September and then allowed to mature until Christmas.

After the final addition cover very tightly and leave to mature.

This is delicious with cream, ice-cream or meringues, and the brandy can be served as a liqueur.

Wassail bowl

Ingredients

3 small red apples
3oz/75g soft brown sugar
$1/2$ pint/300ml dry sherry or white wine
2 pints/1.1 litres brown ale
$1/2$ tsp ground cinnamon
$1/2$ tsp ground ginger
$1/2$ tsp grated nutmeg
Strips of lemon peel
Slices of orange to garnish

In some areas the wassail bowl is used to serve an old-fashioned punch, which is enjoyed over the Christmas period. It was often given to carol singers, or drunk on Twelfth Night (6 January) or the 'old' Twelfth Night, 17 January. It is associated with the blessing of the apple trees used to make cider, and there are several customs connected with this tradition. Wassail, roughly translated, means 'Cheers' or ' Your health', given as a toast. Customs differ around the country and the recipes and proportions may vary from those given here.

Method

Cut through the skin round the centre of the apples. Put them in a large flameproof bowl with the brown sugar and about 4 tablespoons of ale. Cover the bowl and bake in a pre-heated oven 180°C/350°F/gas mark 4 for 20-30 minutes. Remove the apples from the bowl and set them to one side. Put the rest of the ale, the sherry or wine in the bowl with the spices and lemon peel. Simmer on the top of the stove for 5 minutes, add the apples and serve immediately.

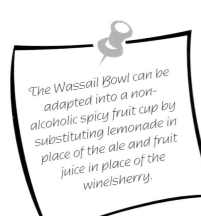

The Wassail Bowl can be adapted into a non-alcoholic spicy fruit cup by substituting lemonade in place of the ale and fruit juice in place of the wine/sherry.

Epiphany

The Feast of the Epiphany is a major Christian festival celebrated on 6 January, though many churches celebrate it on the nearest Sunday. It is a commemoration of the visit of the Magi, or Wise Men, to the infant Jesus, but also celebrates the 'manifestation' of Jesus to the Gentiles, and the fact that his message is for all peoples. The date of 6 January is confused with Twelfth Night, or the day for taking down the Christmas decorations.

In the Greek Orthodox Church Epiphany is celebrated with 'The Blessing of the Waters', recalling the baptism of Christ. After a service a metal cross which has been blessed by a priest is thrown into the sea, and a number of young men dive into the chilly water to retrieve it. The first to reach it is said to have good luck throughout the coming year. This tradition is observed in Margate, Kent, where the service is organized by the Greek Orthodox Church and attended by other Christian clergy, and mayors and civic dignitaries from the area. The Blessing of the Waters is followed by lunch, at which some Greek dishes are served.

The food that was traditionally made for Epiphany celebrations varied around the country. A Twelfth Night Cake seems to have been essential and, again, the recipes varied. In some cases a dried bean and pea were placed in the cake and the man who found the bean was King Bean, and the woman who found the pea was Queen of Misrule; they then led the celebrations at that evening's party. Traditionally the Twelfth Night Cake was large and flat and made of flour, sugar, honey, ginger, pepper, dried fruit and lots of eggs. In northern counties of England Lobscouse and Ponsondie (rich, mulled ale) were enjoyed at Epiphany. In the West Country people look forward to a successful harvest and toast it in warm cider and plum cake.

Lobscouse

Ingredients

To serve about 6 people

1½lb/700g salted silverside of
   beef, soaked overnight
2oz/50g butter or dripping
3lb/1.4kg potatoes, peeled
   and halved
1 carrot, peeled and sliced
1 large onion, peeled and
   quartered
8oz/225g dried peas, soaked in
   cold water overnight
½ tsp chopped thyme
½ tsp chopped mint
1 tsp freshly ground pepper
2 pints/1.1 litres unsalted
   brown stock, warmed

Lobscouse is a stew traditionally eaten by sailors, made usually with mutton, potatoes and vegetables, and thickened with hardtack (ship's biscuits). In the UK the dish was brought to Liverpool by North European sailors, and was known as 'Labskause'. Later this was shortened to 'skause' and then anglicized to 'scouse', the well-known nickname for Liverpudlians.

Method

Trim any skin and fat from the meat and cut the beef into ½in/1.5cm cubes. Melt the butter or dripping in the bottom of a large casserole. Put the potatoes, carrots and onion in the casserole and then put the cubes of meat on top. Drain the peas and put them on top of the beef. Add the thyme, mint and pepper and pour on the stock, adding a little water if there is not enough stock to cover the peas.

Cover with foil or a lid and cook in a pre-heated oven 150°C/300°F/gas mark 2 for 3-4 hours. Serve straight from the casserole.

Ingredients

To serve about 6 people

12oz/350g butter
12oz/350g caster sugar
6 eggs, beaten
12oz/350g plain flour
5 tbsp brandy
1 tsp each of mixed spice,
   ginger, coriander and
   cinnamon
1 1/2 lb/700g mixed dried fruit
2oz/50g flaked almonds

For decoration

3 tbsp apricot jam
2lb/900g marzipan
2lb/900g icing sugar
4 egg whites
1 tbsp lemon juice
2 tsp glycerine
Glacé fruits, angelica, silver
   balls to decorate

A simple but rich variation of the Twelfth Night Cake is to have three circles of puff pastry, cooked, layered together with whipped cream, fresh or tinned fruit and nuts. The top needs then only to be dredged with icing sugar.

Twelfth Night cake

This is suitable for any party when you need a large fruit cake, and without the marzipan, icing and decorations would fit the bill in the West Country for a plum cake to eat with warm cider.

Method

Cream the butter and sugar together until light and fluffy. Gradually add the eggs, flour and spices and brandy alternately, mixing well after each addition. Fold in the fruit and nuts. Tip the cake mixture into a greased and lined 10in/25cm cake tin and bake in a pre-heated oven 150°C/300°F/gas mark 2 for 2 1/2 hours or until the cake is firm and passes the knitting needle test. If the cake starts to brown too much cover it with a sheet of paper about halfway through the cooking time.

Allow the cake to cool in the tin for about 30 minutes before turning it out to finish cooling on a wire rack.

When the cake is cold spread a thin layer of apricot jam over the sides and top. Roll out two-thirds of the marzipan into a long strip, and using the cake tin as a pattern, press it round the cake to give a smooth finish. Now roll out the remaining marzipan and, using the base of the cake tin as a guide, cut a circle of marzipan to fit the top of the cake, pressing it firmly into position.

Leave the marzipan to dry for about 3 days. Now the cake is ready to be iced. Whisk the egg whites lightly until they begin to froth up. Sift and stir in about half the icing sugar, add the lemon juice and the remaining icing sugar and finally stir in the glycerine as this will stop the icing becoming rock-hard. Give the icing a last beat, cover the basin tightly and leave overnight to allow any bubbles to rise to the top. Tip about two-thirds of the icing onto the cake and smooth around the sides and top. Leave the rest of the icing covered in the basin. The next day spread the remaining icing over the cake and roughen the surface with the back of a teaspoon to make small peaks. Finally decorate with glacé fruits, angelica and silver balls.

Greek dishes

Ingredients

To serve about 6 people

2oz/50g long grain rice
Juice of 1 lemon
3 eggs, beaten
2½ pints/1.4 litres hot chicken
  stock
2oz/50g cooked chicken meat,
  finely chopped
2 tbsp parsley, finely chopped
Salt and pepper

Avgolemono

The name 'Avgolemono' comes from two Greek words, one for 'egg' and the other for 'lemon'. Avgolemono is a soup, but it can also be used as a flavouring for other soups or as a sauce for vegetable dishes.

Method

Cook the rice in boiling, salted water for 10-15 minutes. Drain well.

Meanwhile, add the lemon juice to the beaten eggs and mix well. Add about ¼ pint/150ml of the hot stock to this mixture a little at a time, beating well between additions. Bring the remaining stock to the boil, remove from the heat and mix in the chicken and rice. Season with salt and pepper. Whisk in the egg mixture and return to a low heat. Stir continuously and do not allow the soup to boil. Continue to warm the soup for about 5 minutes until it is heated through and has a rich creamy texture. Adjust the seasoning and garnish with the parsley.

Ingredients

To serve about 6 people

2lb/900g aubergines
4 tbsp olive oil
1oz/25g butter
1 large onion, peeled and
    finely chopped
2 cloves of garlic, crushed
1$\frac{1}{2}$lb/700g raw, lean lamb
    mince
1$\frac{1}{2}$lb/700g tomatoes,
    blanched, skinned and
    quartered
1 tsp dried thyme
1 tsp dried rosemary
Salt and pepper
$\frac{3}{4}$ pint/450ml cheese sauce
2oz/50g Parmesan cheese,
    grated

For the cheese sauce

1oz/30g butter
1oz/30g flour
$\frac{3}{4}$ pint/450ml warm milk
1tsp made mustard or mustard
    powder
3oz/75g-90g Cheddar cheese,
    grated
2 egg yolks, well beaten

Moussaka

Although Moussaka is traditionally associated with Greece, it actually originated in the Middle East, and the name is Arabic. Nevertheless it has become a Greek dish today, and recipes vary considerably in different parts of the country and the islands. The dish is complemented by retsina wine.

Method

Soak the unpeeled aubergines, thinly sliced, in salted water for 30 minutes. Drain the slices well and pat them dry on kitchen paper. Heat 2 tablespoons of the oil in a large frying pan, put in a single layer of aubergine slices and fry gently for 1 minute on the first side, 2 minutes on the other side and then 1 minute on the first side. Transfer these to a plate and continue to fry slices of aubergine in a similar way until all are done.

Heat the butter in a large saucepan and fry the chopped onion for 3 or 4 minutes, then add the garlic and the mince. Continue to fry, stirring continuously to brown the meat, for about 5 minutes. Add the tomatoes, thyme and rosemary and simmer for 15-20 minutes.

Meanwhile make the cheese sauce. Melt the butter in a small saucepan, stir in the flour and once this has been absorbed by the butter stir in the warm milk. Continue to cook until you have a smooth sauce, then stir in the mustard followed by the grated cheese. Allow this sauce to cool before stirring in the beaten egg yolks.

Butter an oblong ovenproof dish or tin and put in a layer of aubergines, covered by a layer of meat mixture. Continue with alternating layers, finishing with a layer of aubergines. Cover with the cheese sauce and sprinkle the Parmesan cheese over the top. Bake in a pre-heated oven 150°C/300°F/gas mark 2 for 1 hour or until the top is very crisp and brown. Serve straight from the dish.

Almighty God, who has blessed the earth that it should be fruitful and bring forth whatever is needful for the lives of men and women, prosper, we pray, the work of farmers, and grant such seasonable weather that we may gather in the fruits of the earth, and ever rejoice in your goodness, through Christ our Lord.

Dr Oscar Hardman (adapted)

You have given food to all flesh,
which feeds the young ravens that cry to you
and have nourished us from our youth up:
fill our hearts with good and gladness
and establish our hearts with your grace.

Bishop Lancelot Andrewes (adapted)

Plough Monday

This festival falls on the first Monday after Twelfth Night and traditionally was the day that the farm workers resumed their work after Christmas. However, Plough Monday was treated as a holiday, when decorated ploughs were paraded through the village streets. Money was collected in much the same way as it is at carnival processions today. Originally Plough Monday festivities were based on pagan fertility rites, but when it became a Christian festival the money collected was used to ensure that a Plough Light was kept lit in front of the Ploughmen's Guild altar in the parish church. When this custom died out, the money collected either went towards parochial expenses, or – perhaps more likely – to provide food and drink for the festivities.

Now on Plough Monday or Plough Sunday, in agricultural areas, the day is marked by a special church service. The work of the countryside is offered to the service of God, and a plough is brought into the church to be blessed. Prayers are said for workers on the land, and for a fruitful harvest.

Whilst there are few records of any special food served on this occasion it can be reasonably assumed that fairings and gingerbread (both recipes in St Giles section, see pp. 130,132) would have been eaten. Meals would reflect the harvest of the previous year – perhaps a pot roast or a stew and dumplings (recipes in St Martin section, see pp. 140,141). Rabbit may have been substituted for beef as a more freely available source of meat. All the food would have been washed down with a plentiful supply of local beer and cider.

Rabbit stew and dumplings

Ingredients

To serve about 4 people

4oz/100g streaky bacon
    rashers, chopped, with
    the rind removed
4 rabbit joints
4 celery sticks, washed
    and chopped
8oz/225g carrots, peeled
    and sliced
2 leeks, washed, trimmed
    and sliced
1 bay leaf
2 tbsp wholemeal flour
1 pint/570ml chicken stock
Salt and pepper

This recipe makes a little meat go a long way as the meat is supplemented by adding plenty of vegetables and dumplings.

There is much debate as to who first brought the rabbit to the British Isles – the Romans brought some, but for their own consumption, and any that escaped into the wild would not have survived the cold climate. Following the Conquest in 1066, the Normans constructed warrens on a large scale, and rabbits were carefully managed and provided with the conditions in which they could thrive – which they certainly did! Contrary to tradition, rabbit was not a 'cheap source of meat' for the poor, but a highly prized reserve of the rich.

Young rabbits up to a few months old were relished by monks of the Middle Ages as they decided that they did not count as meat, and could even be eaten on fast days with a clear conscience.

Method

Fry the bacon in a saucepan. When the fat begins to run from the bacon, add the rabbit joints and fry until brown. Add the celery, carrots, leeks and bay leaf, then sprinkle over the flour and stir the meat and vegetables, cooking for a further minute. Remove the pan from the heat and slowly pour in the stock. Return the pan to the heat and bring to the boil stirring all the time. Now transfer the stew to a casserole dish, put on the lid and cook in a pre-heated oven 170°C/325°F/gas mark 3 for about 1½ hours or until the rabbit is tender.

Dumplings

Make the dumplings following the recipe in the St Martin section (p. 141), but substitute 1 tbsp of chopped fresh chives for the parsley and omit the lemon rind.

Twenty minutes before the end of the cooking time place the dumplings in the casserole to cook on top of the gravy.

The stew should be served immediately with additional vegetables.

Plough pudding

Ingredients

To serve 4-6 people

8oz/225g self-raising flour
3oz/75g shredded suet
A good pinch of salt
8 rashers of streaky bacon,
   chopped
1lb/450g sausage meat
1 large onion, peeled and
   chopped
1 tsp chopped sage
$\frac{1}{2}$oz/10g brown sugar
Pork stock or water

This pudding was traditionally made and served on Plough Monday, especially in Norfolk.

Method

Mix the flour, suet and salt together in a mixing bowl and add enough water to form a soft dough. Turn this out onto a floured surface and roll it out to form a circle. Cut out a triangle from this, taking out about a third of the dough that will be used to make the lid of the pudding. Use the larger piece of dough to line a 2 pint/1 litre pudding basin; the dough should fit neatly to line the basin. Now line the dough with the sausage meat, pressing the two layers together.

Mix the bacon, onion, sage and sugar together and put this mixture in the centre of the pudding. Pour in enough stock or water to just cover the contents of the pudding. Roll out the unused dough to form a circle to fit the top of the pudding, sealing the edges firmly. Cover with greaseproof paper and kitchen foil and tie in position tightly with undyed string. Fold a pleat into the covering paper and foil to allow for the pudding to expand during cooking. Steam the pudding for $3\frac{1}{2}$-4 hours. Serve the pudding with a good meaty, thick gravy (see recipe on p. 30) and seasonal vegetables.

Scottish Seed Cakes

In Scotland seed cakes were traditionally served on the first Monday of the new year, which was usually Plough Monday. The recipes for these cakes can be found in the St Catherine's section (p. 149), as they were also eaten on this saint's day.

Gravy

The best gravy is made from the concentrated juices left in the pan after roasting – as this is Plough Monday there may be leftover gravy to be used following a roast Sunday lunch. This recipe will give a good meaty gravy.

Method

To make the gravy, skim the fat off from the top of the meat juices then blend in a tablespoon of flour or cornflour (omit the flour if thinner gravy is preferred).

Stir well over a gentle heat on the hob to give a smooth paste. Slowly add about 1/2 pint/275ml of hot stock, boiling water, wine or sherry. As you stir the gravy over an increasing heat, scrape the bottom of the roasting tin with the spoon to be sure you get any sediment mixed in the gravy – it will help the flavour. If making thinner gravy, boil for 2-3 minutes. For the thickened gravy, boil for 3-4 minutes. Season to taste and skim off any excess fat.

If you prefer darker gravy add a little gravy browning before boiling.

If you prefer highly flavoured gravy, try adding a little yeast or meat extract before the boiling stage.

Collop Monday

Collops

Collops are slices of meat or bacon fried and then gently stewed in gravy. Collop Monday is traditionally the Monday before Ash Wednesday when, especially in Scotland and Northern England, Christians who intended to observe the 'no meat' rule of Lent ate their last meal containing meat until Easter. In Scotland collops were also traditionally eaten on St Andrew's Day as well as Burns' Night – 25 January. In the West Country it was called Peasen or Paisen Monday, when pea soup was eaten.

In the south, collops were generally of ham or bacon, in the north and Scotland steak or lamb were usually used, but venison was also popular.

Collops are best served with creamed potatoes and leeks or cabbage. Rowan or redcurrant jelly makes a good accompaniment to this dish.

Ingredients

To serve about 4 people

$1\frac{1}{2}$lb/700g frying steak or leg of lamb or leg of pork, cut into collops – slices about 2in/5cm x 4 in/10cm x $\frac{1}{2}$ in/1.5cm
1oz/25g seasoned flour
2oz/50g butter
12oz/350g mushrooms, sliced
1 pint/575-600ml brown stock
2 tsp cornflour
Salt and pepper

Method

Toss the collops in the seasoned flour. Melt the butter in a frying pan and fry the mushroom slices. Put the mushrooms in a casserole and fry the collops in the remaining butter for a couple of minutes on both sides. Then place the collops in the casserole on top of the mushrooms. Season with pepper and salt.
Mix the cornflour with a little of the stock, heat the rest of the stock in a saucepan and add the cornflour mixture, stirring all the time until the mixture thickens. Pour the thickened stock over the collops, put the lid on the casserole and cook in a pre-heated oven 180°C/350°F/gas mark 4 for 45 minutes.

Ingredients

1 pint/575ml old garden peas
  or 8oz/225g split peas
1¹/₂ pints/850ml water
1 or 2 sticks of celery, chopped
1 small onion, chopped
Pinch each of ground mace,
  ground cloves and black
  pepper
2¹/₂ pints/1.4 litres good meat
  or vegetable stock
12oz/350g fresh or frozen
  young peas
6 slices French bread and
  clarified butter

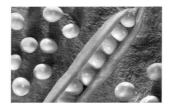

Ingredients

1 tbsp olive oil
6 washed, sliced spring onions
2 peeled, chopped cloves of
  garlic
1¹/₂ pints/850ml vegetable
  stock
1¹/₂lb/600g shelled, fresh or
  frozen peas
1 round lettuce
Large handful chopped mint
Salt and pepper
4 tbsp lightly whipped double
  cream
Sprigs of mint to garnish

Green pea soup

This is a basic soup based on an old recipe.

Method

Use the water to soak the split peas overnight if these are being used. Simmer the split peas or old garden peas in the water together with the celery, onion, mace, cloves and pepper, until tender. Blend this mixture and add to the stock. Just before serving reheat the soup, adding the fresh or frozen peas, and simmer until tender. Serve with the slices of buttered French bread floating in each bowl.

Clarified butter is easily prepared by melting unsalted butter gently in a saucepan. It will foam at first but this will soon reduce. Pour the liquid through a coffee filter paper or just let it stand, and pour off the clear liquid, without the milk solids underneath, into a basin. Without the milk solids the butter will keep for a long time without going rancid.

Pea, spring onion and mint soup

A modern variation of pea soup incorporates more flavours.

Method

Slowly fry the onions and garlic in the olive oil until soft. Pour in the stock, bring to the boil, add the peas and bring back to the boil before lowering the heat to simmer, then stir in the lettuce and mint. Cook until the peas are soft, remove from the heat and blend in a liquidizer. Season. Reheat before serving, adding a swirl of cream and a sprig of mint to each serving.

Shrove Tuesday

Shrove Tuesday follows Collop Monday in the run-up to Lent. It is also called Pancake Day, Bannock Tuesday and Doughnut Day, and in Scotland it has been called Brose Day (brose is a rich savoury broth) – all these foods were eaten in different areas of the country.

In the week immediately before Lent Christians were obliged to go to Confession. 'Shrive' meant to hear Confession and to absolve a person's sins following a penance, hence Shrove Tuesday. Shrovetide used to last for four days, from the previous Saturday up to Shrove Tuesday. In some countries today Shrove Tuesday is regarded as a time for a final fling before Lent, and carnivals and Mardi Gras are organized; in Rio de Janeiro, for example, this lasts for three days.

Basic pancakes

Ingredients

4oz/100g plain flour
2 eggs
$\frac{1}{2}$ pint/275ml milk or milk
   and water
$\frac{1}{2}$ tsp salt
Little butter for frying
Sugar and lemon juice or
   other filling

Pancakes have been cooked and enjoyed for many centuries. Originally the flour and eggs were mixed with water as this was thought to give a lighter pancake. Today it is more usual to use milk or cream. The basic pancake is eaten with sugar and lemon and/or orange juice and is folded in half and in half again. There are endless variations of fillings for pancakes, which can be sweet or savoury. Savoury pancakes are usually rolled not folded. As there are variations of fillings there are also variations of pancake mixture.

Method

Sift the flour and salt into a large bowl, whisk the eggs in one by one and then add the milk, slowly whisking to give a smooth, lump-free mixture.

Grease the surface of an 8in/20cm crêpe/pancake pan or frying pan. Pour in sufficient mixture to thinly cover the surface, cook on a fairly high heat for about a minute, and when the lower surface is brown turn or toss the pancake and cook the other side until it is brown. Turn the pancake out onto a warm plate, add the filling and roll or fold as required. Serve at once or keep warm until the batter mix has all been cooked.

Pancakes can be made in advance and, if separated with sheets of baking paper, frozen.

Shrove Tuesday buns

Ingredients

To serve about 6 people

12oz/350g strong white flour
2oz/50g sugar
1oz/25g fresh yeast
8fl oz/225ml milk, warm
4oz/100g butter, melted
1 egg, beaten
A small quantity of marzipan
1/2 pint/150ml whipping or
  double cream
A little icing sugar for
  dredging

These are luxury cakes which are enjoyed in some parts of the country before the stricter diet of Lent begins.

Method

Place the flour in a mixing bowl and stir in the sugar. Mix the yeast in the warm milk and add this to the flour with the butter. Knead until the dough is smooth and shiny. Cover and leave the dough in a warm place for 1 hour to prove. Knead the dough again and then divide it into 12 equal portions and roll these into balls. Put the balls on a greased baking sheet and leave for a further 20 minutes in a warm place. Brush the cakes with a little of the beaten egg and bake for 15 minutes in a pre-heated oven 200°C/425°F/gas mark 7.

Cool on a wire rack. Cut a triangle from the top of each bun and mould a slice of marzipan to fill the hole.

Pipe some whipped cream around the triangle and replace the cut-out tops, and then dredge the buns with the icing sugar.

Ingredients

To serve 6-8 people

1 1/2 lb/625g neck of mutton or
  shin of beef
4 pints/2 litres water
1 carrot, peeled and chopped
1 turnip, peeled and chopped
1 onion, peeled and chopped
2 leeks, washed, trimmed and
  thinly sliced
3 level tbsp pearl barley
1 tbsp chopped parsley
Salt and pepper

Brose
Method

Cut up the meat and remove any fat. Put it in a large saucepan with the water, salt and pepper, and bring it to the boil and simmer for 1 1/2 hours. Add the vegetables and barley, cover and simmer for a further hour or until the vegetables and barley are soft. Sprinkle the chopped parsley on each bowl as the soup is served.

The recipe can be simplified and speeded up if stock cubes are used and the meat is omitted. More vegetables can be added to make it into a satisfying vegetable broth.

Doughnuts

Ingredients

To make 12 doughnuts

8oz/225g strong white flour
1oz/25g margarine
1 egg, beaten
$^1/_2$oz/15g fresh yeast
1 tsp sugar
2fl oz/50ml milk, warm
Oil for deep frying
Caster sugar for dredging

Bannocks are also connected with Shrove Tuesday – see recipes in the St Brigid section (p. 100)

Although doughnuts are enjoyed throughout the year, in past centuries they were made in great numbers on Shrove Tuesday, especially in Hertfordshire and Bedfordshire. The children in particular called this day 'Doughnut Day'. The recipe given below is a quick and modern version of older recipes.

Method

Sift the flour into a mixing bowl and rub in the margarine, then mix in the beaten egg.

Mix the yeast into the milk with the sugar, pour into the flour and beat well.

Knead in a food mixer for 2 minutes. Turn the dough out onto a floured surface and roll it out to about 1in/2.5cm thick. Cut out 3in/7.5cm rounds and remove the centres with a small cutter. The centres can be re-rolled and cut to make ring doughnuts, or used to make small round doughnuts, in which case you will make 8 rings and 8 small round doughnuts; or the dough can be cut into 12 equal pieces and gently rolled into smaller balls. Put the doughnuts on a greased, warmed baking sheet, cover with greased polythene and put in a warm place for about 30 minutes to rise.

Deep fry in hot oil until golden brown; they turn themselves over when the lower half is cooked. Sprinkle the caster sugar liberally on a piece of greaseproof paper, then remove the cooked doughnuts with a slotted spoon to allow the excess oil to drain, and roll them in the sugar until they are completely coated. Eat as soon as possible.

Ash Wednesday

Ash Wednesday marks the beginning of Lent. In earlier centuries, when people wanted to acknowledge their sins, they wore sackcloth and covered themselves in ashes. The legacy of this is that some Christians receive a small cross of ash on their foreheads during an Ash Wednesday church service. The ashes are produced by burning the previous year's Palm Sunday crosses, and these are mixed with holy water or oil. The custom dates back to around the eighth century.

As might be expected, very little special food is associated with this day but the recipe given over the page is for Plateley Fritters, which were eaten on Ash Wednesdays in Yorkshire.

Plateley fritters

Ingredients

To make about 18 fritters

1lb/450g strong white flour
8oz/225g sugar
2oz/50g currants
2oz/50g sultanas
½ tsp each of salt, pepper
and nutmeg
½oz/15g fresh yeast
1 egg, beaten
½ pint/150ml warm milk

These fritters are similar to Scotch pancakes but that batter lacks the yeast and may also lack the sugar and dried fruit.

Method

Sift the flour into a mixing bowl and add the sugar, currants, sultanas, salt, pepper and nutmeg. Mix the yeast into the warmed milk and add this, together with the beaten egg, to the dry ingredients. Beat the mixture to give a smooth batter. Cover the bowl and leave in a warm place to prove for about 1 hour.

Grease a thick-bottomed frying pan or griddle, and drop tablespoonfuls of the batter onto the hot surface. Cook the fritters on both sides until golden brown.

Lent

The season of Lent lasts for 40 days, and in earlier times was strictly observed as Christians fasted to mirror Jesus' 40 days fasting in the wilderness. This meant only one meal a day and total abstinence from meat; at one time it also included milk, cheese and eggs. Sundays were not included in the fast days. Gradually the strict fasting was relaxed; today many people still give up things such as chocolate or alcohol, though it is as common for people to take up a positive discipline instead.

Lent puddings

In some parts of the country Lent puddings were made or bought especially for weekend teas during this season. The puddings were sometimes called pies or even pudding pies. Originally this delicacy had pastry only on top of the filling – it has now migrated underneath. The filling used to contain suet and lots of spices, but over the years the suet has been lost and a lot of the spices too.

Ingredients

Puff or shortcrust pastry
2oz/50g ground rice
1 pint/600ml milk
4oz/100g sugar
2oz/50g butter
4 eggs
Nutmeg and cinnamon
Lemon rind, grated
4oz/100g currants and mixed peel

Method

Reserve a little of the milk and mix this into a paste with the ground rice. Heat the rest of the milk and pour in the ground rice paste, continuing to heat it. As it thickens add the sugar and butter. Cool the mixture, then add the beaten eggs, spices and lemon peel.

Whilst the rice mixture is cooling, roll out the pastry on a floured surface and line either small patty tins or a flan tin. Scatter the dried fruit over the surface of the pastry and pour in the rice mixture. Bake in a pre-heated oven 190°C/375°F/gas mark 5. Cook until the filling is firm to the touch and beginning to brown.

Lentil and vinegar soup

Ingredients

To serve about 4 people

4oz/100g lentils
2 pints/1.1 litres stock
$\frac{1}{2}$ small cabbage, finely
    shredded
1 small lettuce, finely
    shredded
3 spring onions, trimmed and
    thinly sliced
1 leek, trimmed, washed and
    chopped
1 clove garlic, crushed
2 tbsp flour
Salt and pepper
$\frac{1}{4}$ pint/150ml vinegar
Fresh coriander to garnish
Croutons made from small
    cubes of fried bread

Also known as Good Friday Soup. Vinegar was added to this soup to give it extra bite and to remind the person eating it of the Passion of Christ.

When the soup was eaten on Good Friday it acted as a reminder that when Christ cried out in thirst from the cross he was given a sponge soaked in vinegar.

Method

Boil the lentils in the stock, and just as it comes to the boil add the cabbage, lettuce, spring onions, leeks and garlic. Simmer the lentils and vegetables for about 30 minutes until they are tender.

In a bowl mix the flour, salt, pepper and vinegar and pour this into the soup. Let the soup continue to boil for another couple of minutes. Serve garnished with the fresh coriander and the croutons.

In place of the vegetables given in the recipe, try using two carrots, three sticks of celery and a large potato, then add a curry flavour to the soup.

Lenten stew

Ingredients

8 large onions, peeled and
   sliced
4fl oz/125ml sunflower oil
4oz/100g ground almonds
$1/2$ tsp honey
Salt
$1/4$ pint/150ml white wine
$1/4$ pint/150ml boiling water
8 very thick slices of bread,
   crusts removed, or enough
   slices to fit into the bottom
   of the shallow dish you will
   use to serve the Lenten
   stew.

This was used as a main meal or soup, depending on the amount of liquid used.

Method

Pour the oil into a frying pan and cook the onions gently until they are soft and golden.

Put this pan to one side. Put the ground almonds in a small saucepan. Mix the honey and a pinch of salt in the water and pour it over the ground almonds together with half the wine. Leave this for about 10 minutes, stirring occasionally.

During this time toast the bread lightly. Lay the bread in the bottom of a shallow dish. Add the rest of the wine to the onions and simmer until they are reheated. Heat the almond milk until it is hot, then pour it over the bread, and pile the onions on top.

Leek pie

Ingredients

To serve about 4 people

8 leeks, washed, trimmed and
    cut into 1in/2.5cm slices
4oz/100g bacon, smoked or
    green, chopped, with the
    rind removed
1oz/25g butter
$1/4$ pint/150ml stock
1 bay leaf
Salt and pepper
12oz/350g shortcrust pastry
1 egg, beaten

Leeks have long been used to make tasty meals as
well as being useful sources of vitamins. In the days
when Lent was more strictly observed a leek pie
would be a welcome dinner. You can add bacon to
this recipe if you wish to include meat in it.

Method

Melt the butter in a frying pan, add the bacon pieces and
fry them until the fat runs. Add the leeks and cook them
together for a couple of minutes. Pour enough stock into
the pan to just cover the leeks, add the bay leaf and
seasoning, and simmer for 10-15 minutes. Drain off most
of the liquid and allow the leek pie filling to cool.
Grease a shallow pie dish, about 9in/23cm in diameter,
and roll out the pastry to about $1/4$in/5mm thickness.
Line the pie dish, put in the filling and cover with the
remaining pastry. Trim off any excess pastry and seal the
edges, making a slit in the top to allow steam to escape.
Brush the top of the pie with the beaten egg.
Bake in the centre of a pre-heated oven 190°C/375°F/gas
mark 5 for 30-40 minutes, until the pastry is golden
brown.

Lenten teacakes

Ingredients

To make 10-12 teacakes

1lb/450g strong white flour
1 level tsp salt
1¹/₂oz/40g butter
2oz/50g sugar
¹/₂ pint/300ml milk, warm
1oz/25g fresh yeast
1 50mg vitamin C tablet
2oz/50g sultanas
2oz/50g currants

These are probably a derivative of 'manchet', a medieval loaf made from especially fine flour and shaped by hand, rather like our rolls, and cooked without a tin. There are two versions of the teacake – the plain type was cut open, toasted, buttered and included a savoury filling – but it was the version with fruit in it that was especially made during Lent.

Method

Place the flour and salt in a large mixing bowl, rub in the butter and make a well in the centre. Dissolve the sugar in the milk and mix in the yeast, together with the crushed vitamin C tablet. Pour this liquid into the dry ingredients, mix and knead to form a smooth dough, then work in the dried fruit. The fruit works in more easily if it is warm and slightly damp.

Divide the dough into 3oz/75g pieces, mould them into balls and put them on warmed, greased baking sheets. Flatten the balls, either with the palm of your hand or with a rolling pin. The teacakes should be about 3¹/₂in/9cm discs.

Cover the trays with greased polythene and leave in a warm place to prove for 45-60 minutes. Bake in a pre-heated oven 225°C/435°F/gas mark 7¹/₂ for 10 minutes or until golden brown. They can be brushed with the milk and sugar glaze (details in the Good Friday section, p. 60). For the plain version omit the dried fruit and reduce the sugar to ¹/₂oz/15g. These are very useful when cut in half and filled as sandwiches.

In past centuries Easter or Lenten biscuits were enjoyed by rich and poor alike. The wealthy ate the small glazed cakes on Shrove Tuesday, the last day of rich eating before they started the Lenten fast. For the poor these delicacies were a rare treat. The recipe for the biscuits is to be found in the Easter Day section (p. 63) because today the biscuits are made and eaten at Easter rather than on Shrove Tuesday.

Mothering Sunday

This special day falls on the fourth Sunday in Lent, and was sometimes called 'Simnel Sunday'. Today it is more often known as Mother's Day. Whichever title is used it is seen as a day on which we give thanks for our mothers, and today that includes people who are mother-figures to children, even if they are not blood relatives.

Mothering Sunday also gives Christians an occasion to celebrate the motherhood of Mary, the mother of Jesus. It also used to be a time when parishioners would make every effort to make a pilgrimage to their Mother Church – that is, the cathedral of their Diocese.

Coming six months after new servants were hired at the October fairs of years ago, Mothering Sunday was a convenient time for young people, particularly girls 'in service', to return home to see their families. Sometimes the girls were allowed to make a cake to take home, to demonstrate the cooking skills they had learnt in their post away from home. This is the origin of the Simnel cake, which is not only associated with Mothering Sunday but also with Easter. On the way home the girls picked little posies of wild flowers from the fields and hedgerows, an additional gift for their mothers, and these were the origin of giving posies to children in church to take home to their mothers. The posies also brighten up the church in the middle of Lent, when many churches do not have the usual flower arrangements.

The Simnel cake recipe here is the usual one from the Shrewsbury area with a layer of marzipan through the middle of a good, rich fruit cake. This cake is traditionally topped with a layer of marzipan on which are 11 balls of marzipan to represent the remaining 11 apostles after the crucifixion. As an alternative, the Bury Simnel cake is a flat, spicy cake.

Ingredients

To make an 8in/20cm cake

8oz/225g plain flour
1½ tsp baking powder
1 tsp mixed spice
6oz/175g sugar
6oz/175g butter
3 eggs, beaten
1lb/450g mixed dried fruit
2oz/50g almonds,
    chopped
2oz/50g glacé cherries,
    halved
2oz/50g candied peel
2 tbsp milk
1 large packet marzipan
    (to make marzipan see
    the St Mark section, on
    p. 112)
A little apricot jam

Shrewsbury Simnel cake
Method

Sieve the flour, baking powder and spice together in a bowl. Cream the butter and sugar together, then slowly add the flour to this mixture. Add the eggs one at a time as you work in the flour. Mix in the rest of the ingredients carefully.

Roll out the marzipan and cut out two circles. (It is helpful to use the cake tin base as a guide.) Line the cake tin with non-stick baking paper and spoon in half the cake mixture, flatten the top and press on one of the marzipan circles. Carefully spoon on the rest of the cake mixture and flatten the surface. Bake in a pre-heated oven 150°C/300°F/gas mark 2 for 2-2½ hours. To test that the cake is cooked press lightly with a finger; it should feel firm. (Do not test in the usual way, with a knitting needle or skewer – it will come out sticky because of the warm marzipan.) Allow the cake to cool in the tin for a little while before turning it out to cool on a wire rack.

When the cake is cold spread a thin layer of apricot jam over the top and cover with the second circle of marzipan. (The jam helps to hold the marzipan to the cake.) Place the eleven balls of marzipan around the top edge of the cake. The marzipan can be brushed with egg white and the cake placed under a grill just long enough for the marzipan to begin to brown.

Ingredients

1oz/25g each butter and lard or 2oz/50g butter
5oz/150g plain flour
3oz/75g sugar
½ tsp baking powder
8oz/225g currants
1oz/25g candied peel
½ tsp ground cinnamon
1 tsp ground nutmeg
1 egg, beaten
2-3 tbsp milk
Glacé cherries and whole blanched almonds to
    decorate

Bury Simnel cake
Method

Rub the fat into the flour and stir in the sugar, baking powder, currants, peel and spices. Add the egg to make a very stiff dough, adding the milk if necessary. Form the dough into a round, flat cake and place on a greased baking sheet. Decorate with the cherries and nuts. Bake in a pre-heated oven 200°C/400°F/gas mark 6 for 30 minutes or until golden brown. Cool on a wire rack.

Passion Sunday

This is the fifth Sunday of Lent and marks the beginning of Passiontide. In the past this day has been given various names – Care/Carling/Carle or Carline Sunday, as well as Whirlin' Sunday. Carling Sunday is the only one of these that is still in use, and that is in northern England and Scotland. The 'care' refers to the sorrow of our Lord's Passion. On Passion Sunday pub landlords gave their customers free Carlings, and this dish was also eaten at home to mark the day. Few now keep up this tradition, though some still do in the north of England. In Scotland, Car cakes were traditionally given to mothers, making this a local version of Mothering Sunday.

Whirlin' Sunday, as mentioned above, was one of the names given to this day, because in parts of Cambridgeshire special cakes called Whirlin' cakes were baked. Whirlin' cakes are still made today in the March area; recipes vary slightly depending on who makes them and what their preference is – be it plain little vanilla sponge cakes or with added spice and dried fruit. The important thing is the icing topping with its whirling pattern.

Carlings

Carlings were dried peas, sometimes called white peas, and they gave their name to this dish. The peas are soaked overnight in water seasoned with salt, pepper and perhaps some vinegar. The peas were then drained and fried in butter. They can be served plain, or with sugar and rum.

Car cakes

These are highly spiced pancakes. The basic pancake recipe is in the Shrove Tuesday section on p. 34.

Whirlin' cakes

Ingredients

4oz/100g margarine
4oz/100g caster or granulated
   sugar
5oz/125g self-raising flour
2 eggs
A few drops of vanilla essence
   or a little mixed spice
   and/or 3oz/75g dried fruit

These cakes are made by parishioners of St Ursula's church, where people make a donation in return for a cake and a blessing on Passion (Whirlin') Sunday. The legend behind this is that a 'very good woman' was making cakes for her friends and family with the door open. The devil came in disguised as a man asking for a cake, but she realized who he was and that he wanted her soul as well as a cake. Three times she refused his request. The devil was very cross so he caused a strong wind to whirl her up into the sky and round the church spire. The devil vanished as he thought he had now killed the woman. An angel saw what was happening and rescued the woman, bringing her safely down at her own garden gate. She gave thanks to God for her safe deliverance and the patron saint of the church put it into the hearts of the parishioners to make the whirlin' cakes in remembrance of this.

Method

Place paper cases in patty tins.
Place margarine, sugar, eggs and flour in a bowl and mix well. Add the vanilla essence or spice and fruit and stir in. Place dessertspoonfuls of the mixture in each paper case and bake in a pre-heated oven at 160°C/325°F/gas mark 3 until the cakes are golden.
Cool on a wire rack and when cold ice the tops marking them with a swirling, whirling pattern.

Palm Sunday

Palm Sunday is the Sunday before Easter, when Christians celebrate Jesus' triumphal entry into Jerusalem, riding on a donkey to signify that he came in peace. Jesus' disciples and the crowds welcomed Jesus into the city with shouts of 'Alleluia!' and waving palm branches. This is commemorated in churches by processions – with or without a donkey – and by the distribution of palm crosses to the congregation. Palm Sunday was once also known as Fig Sunday: the custom of eating figs commemorated Jesus' cursing of the barren fig tree on the day following his arrival in Jerusalem. In some churches children were given small packets of figs to eat.

Fig flan
Ingredients

To make an 8in/20cm flan

1lb/450g chopped dried figs
2oz/50g currants
6oz/175g sugar
1 tbsp black treacle
1 tbsp grated orange rind
2 egg whites
$1/2$ tsp mixed spice
8in/20cm flan tin lined with shortcrust
    pastry and baked blind

Method

Whisk the egg whites until they are stiff. Mix all the other ingredients together in a separate bowl then gently fold in the egg whites. Pour the mixture into the flan case and bake in a pre-heated oven 190°C/375°F/gas mark 5 for 20 minutes or until golden brown. Let the flan cool and serve with whipped cream.

An alternative filling

5oz/150g trimmed, chopped dried figs
$3^1/_2$oz/100g fresh white breadcrumbs
6 tbsp black treacle
9 tbsp golden syrup
2 tbsp lemon juice
4oz/125g shelled walnuts or pecan nuts

Method

Scatter figs over the base of the flan. Mix together the breadcrumbs, treacle, golden syrup and lemon juice and add 3oz/75g of the nuts. Spread this mixture over the figs. Decorate with the remaining nuts. Bake in a pre-heated oven 200°C/400°F/gas mark 6 for 20 minutes or until the filling is just firm. Serve with crème fraiche, cream or natural yoghurt when cold.

Fig sly cakes

Rich pastry

10oz/275g plain flour
4oz/100g butter and 3oz/75g
    lard or 7oz/175g butter or
    margarine
2oz/50g caster sugar

For the filling

8oz/225g chopped dried figs
3oz/75g walnut pieces,
    chopped
2oz/50g raisins
2oz/50g currants
A little milk to glaze

These cakes look plain, but the pastry hides the rich figgy filling.

Method

To make the pastry, sift the flour into a bowl, add the fat and rub it into the flour to form a breadcrumb texture. Add sufficient water to bind the mixture together. Chill the pastry whilst the filling is made.

Put the figs, nuts and dried fruit into a saucepan with $1/4$ pint/150ml water and heat, stirring all the time, until the water has been absorbed. Leave this mixture to cool. Divide the dough in half, roll it out and line a shallow tin, 7in/18cm x 11in/28cm, and spread the fruit mixture on the pastry. Roll out the remaining pastry to cover the fruit mixture. Seal the edges well, mark the top into 12 squares, but do not cut through the pastry, and then brush them with a little milk. Bake in a pre-heated oven 190°C/375°F/gas mark 5 for about 40 minutes or until golden brown. Leave to cool, then cut through the marked squares.

Figgy pasties
The above fruit mixture can be used as a filling for small dessert pasties.

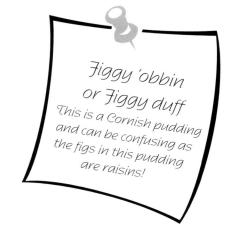

Figgy 'obbin or Figgy duff
This is a Cornish pudding and can be confusing as the figs in this pudding are raisins!

Pax bread

This bread is made for both Palm Sunday and Easter. Make some spicy, fruit dough as for hot cross buns (recipe in the Good Friday section, p. 60) and instead of making buns, mould the letters P A X.

When the bread is cooked and cold it can be decorated with icing and glacé cherries.

Pax cakes

In 1570, Lady Margaret Scudamore, of Kentchurch Court, Herefordshire, arranged for five shillings-worth of cake and nine penn'orth of ale to be distributed to the congregations of four Herefordshire churches on Palm Sunday, in an effort to promote good neighbourliness. Nowadays, instead, 'pax cakes' or biscuits, stamped with an image of the Paschal Lamb and the words 'God and Good Neighbourhood', are distributed to the congregation at the end of the Palm Sunday service.

In some parishes, a large, fairly plain cake with a suitable 'Peace' inscription on it was shared by the congregation who would pass a slice to their neighbours, saying either, 'Peace and good neighbourhood' or 'Peace and goodwill'. In other parishes, baskets of buns, covered with a white cloth, were brought round the congregation by the churchwardens immediately after the collection had been taken. This sharing was regarded as a good way to settle any differences within the church congregation.

This is a tradition that could easily be started in a local church congregation and it was with this in mind that I have included a recipe for Pax biscuits. I used a simple biscuit recipe and with a sharp knife cut the letters P A X on each biscuit before they were cooked. They were individually wrapped and handed to the congregation as they left church. As an alternative, one large Madeira cake would be much easier to make!

Ingredients

To make at least 40 biscuits

4oz/100g caster sugar
4oz/100g butter or margarine
8oz/225g self-raising flour
Vanilla essence
1 egg, beaten

Pax biscuits
Method

Sift the flour into a mixing bowl and rub in the fat until the mixture resembles breadcrumbs, then stir in the sugar and bind the mixture to a stiff dough with a few drops of vanilla essence and some of the egg, as necessary.

Roll out the dough thinly on a floured surface, and cut it into biscuits using a 2in/5cm cutter. Cut into the top surface of each biscuit the letters P A X. Bake on greased or lined baking sheets in a pre-heated oven 180°C/350°F/ gas mark 4 for about 15 minutes until just changing colour. Cool on a wire rack.

Ingredients

6oz/150g butter or margarine
6oz/150g caster sugar
3 eggs
8oz/225g self-raising flour

Madeira cake

A suitable Pax cake.

Method

Prepare a 7in/17.5cm cake tin by lining it with baking paper. Place all the ingredients in a mixing bowl and beat until well mixed and smooth.

Put the mixture in the cake tin and bake in a pre-heated oven 160°C/325°F/gas mark 3 for $1^1/_2$-$1^3/_4$ hours. The cake should be golden brown and firm to the touch. Allow the cake to cool in the tin for about 5 minutes before completing cooling on a wire rack.

Decorate the cake appropriately for a Pax cake.

Maundy Thursday

Maundy Thursday, the day before Good Friday, is the day on which Jesus and the disciples ate the Last Supper in the upper room, the Passover meal which commemorates the night of the first Passover before Moses led the Jewish people out of Egypt. It is the occasion when Jesus gave his disciples his new commandment, 'to love one another'. In Latin the word for commandment is 'mandatum', hence 'Maundy'. It was during this evening that Jesus became the servant of his disciples and washed their feet, a tradition which has been observed through the centuries by popes, kings and bishops. The Pope still washes the feet of 12 people on Maundy Thursday, and the tradition has been revived in recent years in this country, led by the present Archbishop of Canterbury, Rowan Williams. The last monarch in Britain to wash feet was James II; the custom survives today as the monarch's presentation of the Maundy Money.

In the Anglican and Roman Catholic traditions Maundy Thursday sometimes begins with a Chrism Eucharist held in the morning. Chrism is a mixture of oil and balsam and traditionally it is consecrated only by a bishop, on Maundy Thursday. Priests can then use the oil at baptisms, ordinations and confirmations at their own churches through the coming year.

In other churches the tradition of stripping the altar, and the removal from the church of all decorations, hangings and candles, is observed following an evening Eucharist. The stripping of the altar symbolizes the stripping of Jesus for his scourging and crucifixion. The church remains bare until Easter Day.

Jewish Passover meal Pesach Seder

At the Jewish observance of the Passover, Pesach Seder, a total of five traditional questions are asked by the youngest child present, to explain the origins and events of the original Passover. Central to the ceremonies is the Seder Plate on which six symbolic foods are set out. Each represents an episode in the Passover story from Exodus.

Matzo is unleavened bread which plays an important part in the meal. It is made from special flour using grain that at no time becomes damp; neither does the flour until it is made into dough. The dough is cooked for just 18 minutes. All these precautions are to ensure that no fermentation takes place. The six symbolic foods are:

1. **Charoset** is a mixture of apples, nuts, wine and spices, and is symbolic of the mortar used by the Israelites in their building for the Egyptians. The mixture of nuts, apples and spices is moistened with wine, and the texture should be reminiscent of mortar.
2. **Zeroa**, a shankbone or neck of poultry, roasted. Zeroa is a reminder of the strength of God who brought the Israelites out of slavery, and it is also symbolic of the paschal lamb offered as the Passover sacrifice in the Temple in Jerusalem.
3. **Baytzah** is a hard-boiled egg, symbolic of the regular festival sacrifice brought to the Temple. Some authorities see this as the symbol of mourning for the two Temples which were destroyed, once by the Babylonians in 586 BC and again by the Romans in 70 AD. The egg symbolized the loss of the Temples, and so became the food of mourning.
4. **Karpas**, a vegetable such as celery or potato, is dipped in salt water and represents tears. The custom of serving this as the Passover meal dates back to first-century Jerusalem when it was usual to begin a meal by serving vegetables as hors d'oeuvres.
5. **Maror** is a bitter herb – usually horseradish root or prepared horseradish. Maror represents the bitter life of slavery endured by the Israelites in Egypt.
6. **Charzeret** is a bitter vegetable, such as celery or lettuce. Those who do not include charzeret on the Seder Plate sometimes put a dish of salt water there instead.

A Christian Passover Service

Introduction

The Seder Dish is before the celebrant.
The celebrant washes his/her hands then distributes parsley and salted water for all to eat, saying:

'Blessed art thou, O Lord our God, King of the Universe, Creator of the fruit of the earth.'

Some wine is poured for all and some is set aside.

The celebrant continues, saying:

'Blessed art thou, O Lord our God, King of the Universe, Creator of the fruit of the vine. Blessed art thou, O Lord our God, King of the Universe, who has kept us alive and sustained us to reach this season.'

Everybody drinks a sip of wine.

The celebrant takes a matzo from the middle of the plate, divides it in two then places the smaller section between the other matzos and sets the larger piece aside. The Seder Dish is raised, saying:

'This is the bread of affliction which our forefathers ate in the land of Egypt. Everybody who is hungry, let them come and eat; everybody who is in need let them come in and celebrate the Passover.

The traditional question

Why is this night different from all other nights?

We were slaves to Pharaoh in Egypt; the Lord our God brought us out from there with a mighty hand and outstretched arm. For the Holy One planned the end of bondage to fulfil the promise he made to Abraham that 'your seed shall be a stranger in a land that is not yours and you shall serve them, and afterwards they shall come out'.

On this night our Lord Jesus Christ, the promised Messiah, instituted the sacrament of his body and blood and offered himself to God for our salvation, opening the gates of heaven to all.

The Lord brought us forth out of the land of Egypt with a mighty hand and outstretched arm and with signs and wonders. For these are the 10 plagues which he brought upon the people in Egypt: blood, frogs, lice, beasts, boils, blight, hail, locusts, darkness and the slaying of the first-born.

He chose a young woman from among us, his people, and sent his only son, true God and true man, who lived our human life, suffered and died for us on the cross.

Everybody drinks a sip of wine.

Four questions

Why do we eat lamb on this night, what is its significance?

It is to remind us when God slew the first-born of the Egyptians. He commanded our forefathers to roast a lamb and eat it and sprinkle their door posts with its blood so that these houses were 'passed over' by God and their first-born not slain. Jesus Christ our Lord offered himself as the Paschal Lamb to save us from our sin. As St John says, 'Here is the Lamb of God who takes away the sin of the world.'

Lamb is no longer eaten but symbolized to recall the days of the Temple.

Why do we eat matzo, unleavened bread, on this night?

It is first of all in memory of the flight of our forefathers from Egypt when there was no time for their dough to become leavened. It was this unleavened bread that our Lord Jesus Christ took at the Passover; or on the night in which he was betrayed, he took bread, gave thanks, broke it, and gave it to his disciples, saying, 'Take, eat, this is my body which is given for you; do this in remembrance of me.

Some matzo is eaten.

Why do we drink wine on this night, what is its significance?

Wine was drunk by our forefathers to celebrate the delivery from Egypt and it was this wine which our Lord took at the Passover. After supper he took the cup and gave thanks; he gave it to them, saying, 'Drink this, all of you; this is my blood of the new covenant which is shed for you and for many for the forgiveness of sins. Do this, as often as you drink it, in remembrance of me.'

Everybody drinks a sip of wine.

Why do we eat bitter herbs, what is their significance?

When our ancestors were slaves in Egypt the Egyptians embittered their lives with hard labour and oppression, causing them to shed many tears. The bitterness of labouring, suffering and death Christ took upon himself. We, too, must work out our salvation in labour and suffering, for 'if any want to become my followers, let them deny themselves and take up their cross and follow me'.

Bitter herbs are eaten, followed by the sweet.

The eternal message of Passover

In every generation it is right to remember how God saves his people from slavery, slavery from the destructive forces in our hearts and lives.

The cup of wine is raised.

And so we give thanks to him who brings us out of slavery into freedom, from darkness into light, from rejection into redemption.

Everybody drinks a sip of wine.

Share together hymns/songs, prayers of intercession and Holy Communion.

The celebrant concludes, saying:
'Almighty and most wonderful God; God of Abraham, Isaac and Jacob; in partaking of this Paschal supper we have remembered both your goodness to our ancestors in the Old Testament and recalled that at the Last Supper Jesus Christ shared with his disciples the night before he died, leaving us a memorial of his passion and death. May we so partake of this Seder year by year, that we may evermore be conscious of your overflowing goodness to us through Jesus Christ our Lord. Amen.'

Blessing

Passover meringues

During the week of Passover – when the Jews celebrate the Exodus from Egypt – the Jews do not eat any leaven flour, so this is one of the delicious alternatives. These meringues stay in good condition for several days if kept in an airtight tin.

Ingredients

5 egg whites
15oz/375g icing or caster sugar
10oz/250g raisins
5oz/125g chopped nuts

Method

Whisk the egg whites until they are stiff. Add the sugar a spoonful at a time and beat until stiff after each addition of sugar. Fold in the nuts and raisins. Put small spoonfuls of the meringue on greased or lined baking sheets. Cook for about 30 minutes, until crisp, in a pre-heated oven 150°C/300°F/gas mark 2.

Agape meal

When the first Christians obeyed Jesus' command to remember him in the sharing of bread and wine, some of them did so in the context of a full meal, the Love-feast or Agape. Christians were condemned for this practice, as it was thought to be simply an excuse for over-indulgence. Some church congregations have revived the Agape meal, which is combined with a Eucharist on Maundy Thursday night. Below is an outline for such an event.

President: Christ Jesus, being found in human form, humbled himself: and became obedient even to death, death on a cross (Phil. 2.8). The Lord be with you.

All: **And also with you.**

President: We meet together to share in the Agape, the feast of Christ's love. In accordance with the earliest custom of the Church, we celebrate the Christian Passover with the Lord. As his first disciples were with Jesus at his Last Supper when they shared the Passover meal of fellowship, so we also as Christ's disciples come together.

Hymn

President: Let us prepare ourselves to share the Christian Passover by asking forgiveness of the sin that is within each of us, and mars our fellowship with each other.

All: **Confession**

President: **Absolution and Collect for Maundy Thursday**

Old Testament reading
Gospel reading
Sermon
Hymn such as 'Meekness and majesty'
The meal is now eaten (suggested ingredients given below) or just the main course.
Intercessions
The Peace
The sweet can be eaten here.
Hymn such as 'A new commandment'
Eucharistic Prayer
The Lord's Prayer
Communion – *the bread and wine are passed round the gathered congregation, each administering to the next.*
Prayer of thanks
Hymn such as 'Be still, for the presence of the Lord'
President: Come now: let us leave (John 14.31).
All: Amen
The people clear the room and leave in silence.

Suggested main meal

Cold lamb, hard-boiled egg, lettuce and matzo with a small amount of butter.
The sweet can simply be an apple.
Red grape juice is an acceptable drink.

Good Friday

Many years ago the three days leading up to Easter – Maundy Thursday, Good Friday and Holy Saturday, were called Still Days. In Germany Good Friday is still known as 'der stille Freitag', or Silent Friday. The name probably derives from 'God's Friday'; the Anglo-Saxons referred to 'Long Friday'.

Good Friday is not as widely observed as it once was in past years, though many Christians now take part in 'walks of witness' and make a more public affirmation of their faith.

Many churches also hold a three-hour service of prayer, meditation and sacred music. At one time the only shops open were the fishmonger's (since many people ate only fish on Good Friday), and the baker's, for hot cross buns.

Lentil and vinegar soup is also known as Good Friday soup and a recipe can be found in the Lent section (p. 40).

Fig dishes are served on this day – see the recipes in the Palm Sunday section (pp. 49-50).

Fig-Sue

This was traditionally served in Lancashire on Good Friday. It is made from ale, bread, figs and nutmeg, boiled together to a soup consistency and eaten hot. No detailed recipe could be traced.

Ingredients

1 cup fresh parsley, chopped
1 clove garlic, crushed
Lemon juice
Salt and pepper
4 St Peter's fish, (John Dory) filleted
Seasoned flour
Cooking oil
1 onion, chopped

Saint Peter's fish (John Dory) with parsley sauce

When John Dory is not readily available trout or bass are suitable substitutes for this recipe. It is an easy meal to make quickly.

Method

In a food processor blend the parsley, garlic and about 4 tablespoons of water until the resultant sauce is smooth. Add lemon juice, salt and pepper to taste. Prepare the fish fillets by coating them in the seasoned flour, then heat some cooking oil in a pan and fry the fish until it is brown on both sides. Remove the fish to a warm serving dish, put the onion in the pan and cook until it begins to brown, then add the prepared parsley sauce to the pan and cook for a couple of minutes. Pour the sauce over the fish and serve with seasonal vegetables.

Ingredients

1lb/400g strong white flour
1 tsp salt
1/2 tsp mixed spice
2oz/50g sugar
1oz/25g fresh yeast
1 50mg vitamin C tablet
8fl oz/200ml warm milk
1 egg
4oz/100g dried fruit
For the crosses use 4oz/100g pastry or a thick batter made of 1 egg and 4oz/100g flour and a little milk or water if needed.
For the glaze use 2 tbsp sugar dissolved in 4 tbsp milk

Hot cross buns
Method

Sift the flour, salt and spice into a bowl, and stir in the sugar. Dissolve the yeast and the crushed vitamin C tablet in the warm milk, then add this and the egg to the dry ingredients. Mix well and knead for about 2 minutes in a food mixer (longer if by hand). Work in the dried fruit. This is easier if the fruit is warm and damp. If added early the fruit may well be mashed.

Divide the dough into equal sized pieces about 3oz/75g and roll into buns, then place on a greased or lined baking sheet, allowing space for the dough to expand. Leave in a warm place covered with greased polythene until the buns are twice their original size. Now pipe on the batter or pastry strips to form the crosses, or, you can cut the crosses into the dough. Bake in a pre-heated oven 240°C/475°F/gas mark 9 for 6 or 7 minutes. Glaze the buns as soon as they come out of the oven. For an alternative glaze use warmed golden syrup. Cool the buns on a wire rack.

Easter Day

Alleluia! Christ is risen He is risen indeed – alleluia!

Easter Day, when Christians celebrate Jesus' resurrection from the dead, is a day for rejoicing. Church services range from Dawn Walks to special Eucharists and other celebration services. Easter is a movable feast and can be any date from 22 March to 25 April. The actual date each year is the Sunday following the first full moon after the Spring Equinox. The method of calculating Easter was the cause of some dissension between Celtic Christians and Roman Christians, whose method of calculation was decided by the Council of Nicea in 325. This method was adopted by all British Christians at the Synod of Whitby in 664.

When the strict fast of the six weeks of Lent is over the celebrations at Easter have real significance – not least in the giving and receiving of chocolate Easter eggs!

Easter Day menu

Breakfast	Boiled eggs variously decorated by both children and adults.
Lunch	Roast lamb or chicken and seasonal vegetables followed by apple tansy (see recipe in this section) is suggested.
Tea	Some recipe ideas for a celebration tea are given here.

Roast lamb

The leg is the best joint of lamb for roasting, especially for feeding a family, as there is no waste except for the bone. Choose a short and thick leg. The shoulder is also a good roasting joint and is cheaper than leg, although the meat is sweeter and fattier. Roast the joint at 180-190°C/350-375°F/gas mark 4 or 5, allowing 20 minutes per lb/450g plus 20 minutes. Serve with a selection of vegetables according to availability and likes and dislikes; roast potatoes are usually popular and mint sauce and gravy are 'musts' as accompaniments to the lamb.

Apple tansy

Ingredients

To serve about 4 people

1lb/450g dessert apples, peeled, cored and sliced
2oz/50g butter
4oz/100g caster sugar
$1/2$ tsp ground cloves
4 eggs, separated
4 tbsp double cream

On Easter Sunday some families served a tansy pudding, a dessert that has been greatly altered over the years. Tansy is a yellow-flowered herb with medicinal properties and a bitter flavour, and was originally used as a flavouring. By the sixteenth century the tansy dish had changed into a sweet-tasting omelette, not containing any of the herb, and by the seventeenth century it had become largely what it is today – a creamy fruit and egg purée.

For apple and damson tansy, add 8oz/225g of damsons halved, stoned and quartered. Add the damsons to the apples and complete the dish as given above.

Method

Put the apples and butter in a shallow flameproof dish 10in/25cm in diameter. Cook over a gentle heat (add water if they threaten to burn) until they are pulpy. Remove from the heat and stir in the cloves, rosewater and half the sugar. Beat the egg yolks with 1oz/25g of the sugar and all the cream. Whisk the egg whites until they are stiff, fold them into the egg yolk mixture and then fold this into the apples. Cook over a low heat, stirring gently until the tansy is set. Put the dish under a hot grill to brown and sprinkle the top with sugar. Serve at once with cream.

Easter bunny biscuits

Ingredients

3oz/75g soft margarine
4oz/100g caster sugar
1 egg
8oz/225g plain flour
2 tsp mixed spice
1 pinch of salt
1oz/25g currants

For the glaze

Egg white
Desiccated coconut
Currants

> These are for the children and they may like to help make them.

Method

Cream the margarine and sugar together until light and fluffy. Add the egg and mix well, then sift in the flour, spice and salt and stir. Add the currants and mix to form a stiff dough.

Roll out the dough on a floured surface to be about 1/4in/5mm thick. Cut out the biscuits using a rabbit-shaped cutter, brush the upper surface with egg-white and dip in the desiccated coconut.

Add a currant to represent the eye. Place the biscuits on a greased or lined baking sheet and bake in a pre-heated oven 190°C/375°F/gas mark 5 for about 15 minutes. Remove the biscuits carefully and cool on a wire rack.

Ingredients

3oz/75g butter
3oz/75g caster sugar
1 egg, separated
2oz/50g currants
1/2oz/15g candied peel
1 generous pinch of
    mixed spice
6oz/175g plain flour
A little milk
For the glaze
Caster sugar

Easter biscuits
Method

Cream the butter and sugar together until the mixture is light and fluffy. Add the egg yolk, currants, peel, spice and sifted flour, and mix to a stiff dough with a little milk.

Roll the dough out thinly on a floured surface and cut into biscuits 3in/7.5cm in diameter using a fluted or plain cutter.

Place the rounds on greased or lined baking sheets and bake for 15-20 minutes in a pre-heated oven 180°C/350°F/gas mark 4.

After 10 minutes brush the biscuits with the egg white and sprinkle with caster sugar, then return them to the oven until they are a light golden brown. Remove from the baking sheets and cool on a wire rack.

Easter cake

Ingredients

6oz/150g self-raising flour
4oz/100g caster sugar
4oz/100g butter
4oz/100g sultanas
2oz/50g candied peel
1oz/25g flaked almonds
2 eggs
1 tbsp milk
$1/2$ tsp baking powder
Grated rind of half a lemon

For the icing

6oz/150g icing sugar, sieved
A little lemon juice
A few drops of green
   colouring

This is a plainer alternative to a Simnel cake, traditionally eaten in the northern counties of England at this time.

Method

Cream the butter and sugar until light and fluffy, add the eggs and flour alternately, then add the baking powder, fruit, peel, lemon rind and almonds, and finally add the milk. Tip the cake mixture into a greased and lined cake tin and bake in a pre-heated oven 150°C/300°F/gas mark 3 for 1 hour or until cooked through and golden brown. Cool and store in an airtight tin for a couple of days before decorating with the green icing. Once this has set decorate with suitable Easter cake decorations and an Easter cake frill.

Simnel cake

See recipes in the Mothering Sunday section, p. 46.

Decorate the cake with the marzipan balls representing the apostles and in the centre make a 'nest' of small chocolate Easter Eggs.

Jersey wonders

Ingredients

12oz/350g self-raising flour
4oz/100g plain flour
4oz/100g sugar
4oz/100g butter
4 eggs, beaten
Oil for deep-frying

These were once an Easter speciality, but like hot cross buns are now to be found throughout the year. As with many dishes, there are several local variations, but they are always deep-fried. Some contain cooking brandy; some are served hot with a fruity sauce. Jersey wonders keep well in an airtight tin.

Method

Sift the two flours together and stir in the sugar, then rub in the butter until the mixture resembles breadcrumbs. Add the eggs and mix thoroughly, and knead the mixture until it becomes a stiff, smooth dough – add a little extra flour if the dough is too soft.
Divide the dough into 18 equal sized balls and leave to rest for 20-30 minutes.
Roll the balls into strips about $1/4$in/5mm thick.
Make a slit in the middle of each strip, and bring the two ends round and tuck them through the slit.
Deep-fry the Jersey wonders until they are golden brown. Place them on kitchen paper to remove any excess oil, and then on a wire rack to cool.

Strawberry fritters

Ingredients

1lb/450g large, dry
    strawberries
6oz/175g plain flour
2oz/50g caster sugar
2 tsp grated nutmeg
2 eggs, beaten
8fl oz/225ml single cream
Oil for deep-frying
Sugar to garnish

Plain fritters made from ale, flour and eggs were often eaten at Easter. These strawberry fritters are rather special – now that fruits no longer have to be eaten in season and are readily available throughout the year in supermarkets. Other fresh fruit can be used – pineapple and apple work especially well.

Method

The strawberries are more easily handled if the stalks are left on.

Sift the flour into a bowl and stir in the sugar and nutmeg. Make a well in the middle and drop in the eggs and cream. Stir until all the flour has been gradually drawn into the batter.

Allow the batter to stand for 1 hour.

Heat the oil so that it is hot enough for the fritters to puff up, but not so hot that they brown too quickly.

Dip each strawberry into the batter until it is completely coated and cook a few at a time. You may need to add a little more oil.

Cook until the fritters are golden brown then remove using a slotted spoon. Drain on kitchen paper and keep them warm until all are cooked.

Pile the finished fritters into a pyramid and sprinkle them with sugar.

Easter Monday

The Easter celebrations continue on Easter Monday with various events, many of them outdoors, despite the British weather! Some foods were traditionally enjoyed on this day, such as hare pie (now more likely to be mutton, steak or rabbit pie) and in parts of Gloucestershire fried elvers, or eels.

Eels and elvers were once widely eaten, especially in inland districts. Sea fish would have been an unknown luxury unless it was dried or salted, though this fish would have been quite inedible to us today. Rents were often paid in elvers and eels; in the tenth century the Abbot of Ely received thousands of eels in payment of rent for properties on the monastery's vast estates. They formed easy currency for watermill owners.

Many eel dishes are best bought ready-made. Eels or elvers are sold by fishmongers who keep them alive, as the flesh deteriorates rapidly once the eel is dead. Your fishmonger will skin and clean the eels for you. Recipes using eels include jellied eel, still enjoyed today, eel pie, eel soup, fried and smoked eels. Two recipes for eel are given in this section.

Eel and parsley soup
Method

Ingredients

To serve 6 people

1 pint/600ml fish stock
1 pint/600ml water
$1/4$ tsp ground mace
Small piece of lemon zest
8 black peppercorns
Bouquet garni
Salt
1lb/450g small eels
2oz/50g butter
2 large onions, peeled and
    chopped
3 tbsp plain flour
$1/2$ pint/300ml milk
2 egg yolks, beaten
$1/4$ tsp sugar
4 tbsp finely chopped
    parsley

Put the stock, water, mace, lemon zest, peppercorns and bouquet garni in a large saucepan. Season with salt and bring to the boil, then add the eels. Simmer for 20-30 minutes or until the eels are tender and the flesh begins to come away from the bone. Strain and keep the cooking liquid.

Discard the lemon peel, peppercorns and bouquet garni. Remove the eel flesh from the bones and cut into pieces about $1 1/2$in/4cm in size.

Heat the butter in another saucepan and cook the onion in it over a low heat until it is transparent, stir in the flour and gradually blend in the cooking liquid and milk. Stir continuously as the soup thickens over a moderate heat. Add the pieces of eel and simmer for a further 3 minutes.

Blend about 3 tablespoonfuls of soup with the egg yolks. Add this mixture to the soup with the sugar and stir over a low heat for 2 minutes. The soup will curdle if you let it boil at this stage. Stir in the parsley, check the seasoning and serve immediately.

Fried elvers
Method

Ingredients

To serve 4 people

1lb/450g whole elvers
2 tbsp lard
8 long streaky bacon
    rashers with rinds
    removed
3 large eggs, beaten
Salt and pepper

Rinse the elvers in salted water two or three times until you are sure they are clean, then drain and dry them.

Melt the lard in a frying pan and fry the bacon until crisp. Remove the rashers from the pan and arrange them round a warmed dish.

Add the elvers to the fat in the pan and stir them round until they turn white, which will take only a few seconds.

Pour in the egg, season and stir until the egg has just set. Tip this mixture into the centre of the bacon ring and serve at once.

Mutton pie

Ingredients

To serve 4-5 people

2lb/900g lean mutton or lamb
2 onions, peeled and cut into
  chunky pieces
1lb/450g turnips or carrots,
  peeled and sliced
1oz/25g butter
1oz/25g plain flour
Salt and pepper
12oz/350g shortcrust pastry
1 dssp fresh chopped parsley

These pies are simple to make and are a good stand-by, perhaps for a picnic, if made in advance and stored in the freezer.

Method

Trim the fat from the meat and cut it into cubes of about 1in/2.5cm. Put the meat and vegetables in a saucepan with sufficient water to cover them, and cook over a gentle heat until the meat is tender. (This could take a couple of hours, depending on the quality and size of the meat cubes.)

Remove the pan from the heat, drain off the stock and reserve it. Let the meat and vegetables cool.

Melt the butter in a smaller saucepan, stir in the flour and gradually add the stock to make a rich gravy, then season with salt and pepper.

Line a suitable dish with just over half the shortcrust pastry. Put the cooled meat and vegetables in the pie dish, sprinkle on the parsley and pour on sufficient cooled gravy to three-quarters fill the pie. If the meat and gravy are hot they will spoil the pastry.

Brush round the edges of the pastry with water, cover the pie with a pastry lid and press the edges together to make a good seal. Use the prongs of a fork to press the edges together and give a decorative finish. Cut two slits in the centre of the lid to let the steam out, and decorate the top with pastry leaves.

Brush the top of the pie with milk and bake in a pre-heated oven 200°C/400°F/gas mark 6 for 25 minutes until golden brown. Serve hot or cold with a selection of vegetables.

Easter Fair buttons

Ingredients

8oz/225g plain flour
6oz/150g butter
8oz/225g sugar
1 egg

These biscuits are a variation on shortbread. The recipe can be readily adapted and flavoured with spices such as ginger. The biscuits used to be sold at Easter Fairs, especially in Norfolk.

Method

Rub the butter into the flour, stir in the sugar and mix into a dough with the egg. Roll out thinly on a floured surface and cut into rounds. Place on a greased or lined baking sheet and bake in a pre-heated oven 180°C/360°F/gas mark 4 for 10 minutes until golden brown.

Rogationtide

Rogation Sunday occurs on the Sunday before Ascension Day, and Rogationtide includes the three days following. Rogation derives from 'rogare', the Latin verb 'to ask', and is a time when rural communities asked a blessing on their crops and future harvest. The days of Rogationtide were also known as Gang Days, from the Anglo-Saxon word 'gangen', meaning 'to go', and were days for 'beating the bounds', or in other words marking the limits of the parish boundaries. The event was attended by the village priest and other dignitaries, making it an official community event.

In some coastal towns today, such as Hastings, the local clergy go out in a boat (an RNLI lifeboat in this case) to bless and to pray for a rich harvest from the sea. The Blessing of the Sea in some ports, for example, Colchester in Essex, Whitstable, Kent and Bude, Cornwall takes place during the summer months. The Blessing of the Nets at Brighton, East Sussex and the Blessing of the Boats at Whitby, North Yorkshire take place (or used to take place) at various times of the year.

In Colchester the service is on either the last Friday in August or the first Friday in September. The custom dates back to the sixteenth century when services were held at the opening and closing of the oyster-dredging season. Today the service marks the start of the season. The Mayor, his chaplain and accompanying guests board a boat which is anchored in the River Colnes whilst the chaplain conducts the service and the Mayor makes the first dredge.

Gingerbread and gin are then consumed by the assembled company. (Gingerbread was widely available at most celebrations or festivities as it was originally made from readily available breadcrumbs, ginger and honey.) Once back on land the mayoral party are served a luncheon of freshly dredged oysters and other seafood dishes in the building where oysters are prepared for market.

A recipe for gingerbread is in the St Giles section (p. 132).

A recipe for oysters in cream sauce is in the St Patrick section (p. 109).

Bless, O Lord, the plants, the vegetation, and the herbs of the field, that they may grow and increase to fullness and bear much fruit. And may the fruit of the land remind us of the spiritual fruit we should bear.

Coptic Orthodox Liturgy, Egypt

Blessed be thou, Lord God,
who bringest forth bread from the earth
and makest glad the hearts of thy people.

Ancient Hebrew prayer

Ascension Day

Ascension Day falls on a Thursday, 40 days after Easter. On this day Christians remember Jesus taking the apostles to a mountain and taking his leave of them, ascending into heaven and out of their sight.

Whilst no foods seem to be particularly associated with Ascension Day, some cakes can be suggested to help remember what happened – these suggestions rely on the shape of hills and mountains with snow on the summit.

A dariole mould is a small metal mould about 3in/8cm high with a narrower bottom than top. They are used for a variety of individual portion-sized servings of foods, such as puddings, sweet or savoury mousses and jellies and for portions of rice and mashed potato. They are also known as Madeleine tins.

Sponge mountains
Ingredients

To make 12 'mountains'

4oz/100g butter or margarine
4oz/100g caster sugar
2 eggs
4oz/100g self-raising flour
Jam and desiccated coconut or white icing
  to decorate

Method

Prepare 12 dariole moulds by lightly greasing them. Cream the butter and caster sugar together until light and fluffy. Whisk the eggs and add them, a little at a time, to the creamed mixture, beating well. Very lightly fold in the sieved flour to give a soft dropping mixture. Add a little hot water if necessary to give the right consistency. Half fill each dariole mould and bake in a pre-heated oven 190°C/375°F/gas mark 5 for 12-15 minutes or until the cakes are golden brown and firm to the touch. Leave the cakes to cool in the moulds for 5 minutes and then turn them out to finish cooling on a wire rack. Warm the jam, and brush the top half of each cake with it, then dip the top of the cake in the coconut. Or decorate with white icing.

Ingredients

2 egg whites
2oz/50g granulated sugar
2oz/50g caster or icing sugar

Meringue mountains
Method

Prepare a baking sheet by lining with baking paper.
Place the egg white in a grease-free bowl and whisk until stiff and dry. Whisk in the granulated sugar and continue to whisk until it is as stiff as before. Now fold in the caster or icing sugar using a metal spoon. Pipe to form mountains and dry them out in a very cool oven for 3-4 hours.

Coconut pyramids

These are made of desiccated coconut and condensed milk, the stiff mixture being shaped appropriately and cooked in a moderate oven to harden the outside.

Whitsun

Whitsun, or Pentecost as it is now more widely known, is celebrated 50 days after Easter (the Greek word 'pente' means 50). The term 'Whitsun' is thought to be a corruption of 'White Sunday', and was originally the day when people who had been baptized at Easter wore white to church. Pentecost celebrates the day when the apostles received the Holy Spirit, accompanied by tongues of fire and rushing winds, as they waited and prayed together in Jerusalem. Empowered by the Spirit, the apostles began their great missionary work to spread the gospel and founded the Christian Church – thus Pentecost is the Church's birthday.

Pentecost is also the name of the Jewish festival of 'Shavout' or Spring Harvest, 50 days after the Passover, which celebrates the first fruits of the field, especially early wheat. It also commemorates the giving of the law to Moses on Mount Sinai. The Jewish celebrations at this time include cheese dishes (while Moses was receiving the Law on the mountain, the Hebrews' milk turned to cheese) and mountain-shaped cakes.

At St Briavels in Gloucestershire there is a celebration of Pentecost which dates back some 700 years. Baskets of bread and cheese (Double Gloucester, I hope) are taken to a narrow lane near the church of St Mary by a local forester and after Evensong he throws pieces of bread and cheese from the top of the wall to the congregation waiting in the lane. This custom used to take place inside the church, when the bread and cheese were thrown from the galleries onto the congregation below. In 1857 the ceremony was moved outside into the churchyard, when the bread and cheese was thrown from the church tower. The scramble for the food led to graves being damaged and thus the ceremony was moved to its present site. This may seem a rather silly bit of fun, but it once had a useful purpose; tradition has it that as long as this takes place the commoners retain their rights of grazing and cutting wood in the local Hudnall Wood. In the past it may also have been a way of giving food to the poor.

Some dishes traditionally eaten at Pentecost include cheesecake, baked custard and gooseberry flan and pie.

Ingredients

To serve 6 people

1lb/450g gooseberries,
  topped and tailed
2 heads of elderflowers
6 tbsp white wine
4 tbsp clear honey, warmed
2 eggs, beaten
A pinch of salt
A pinch of nutmeg
$1/4$ pint/125ml double cream
An 8in/20cm flan ring or tin lined
  with shortcrust pastry and baked
  blind (4oz/125g shortcrust pastry
  should suffice)

Gooseberry flan
Method

Put the fruit, elderflowers and wine in a saucepan, cover and very gently simmer until the fruit is tender. This will take about 20 minutes.

Remove the elderflowers and stir the mixture before liquidizing, or alternatively the mixture can be sieved. Add the warmed honey, beaten eggs, salt, nutmeg and cream to the gooseberry mixture. Stir well and pour into the pastry case.

Bake for about 40 minutes in a pre-heated oven 190°C/375°F/gas mark 5 or until the filling is firm and golden brown. Cool on a wire rack and serve with more cream.

Baked custard

Ingredients

To serve 4-6 people

1 pint/600ml single cream or
  $3/4$ pint/450ml milk and
  $1/4$ pint/150ml double cream
1 vanilla pod
4 eggs
2oz/50g granulated sugar
$1/2$ tsp grated or ground
  nutmeg (optional)

Baked custards, made from sherry, cream, eggs and sugar, used to be very rich and only for the wealthy. Baked custards today are simpler, but are still best made with cream or a mixture of milk and cream. They are delicious eaten alone or served with fresh fruit, especially strawberries and raspberries.

Method

Gently heat the cream or cream and milk with the vanilla pod until it just reaches boiling point. Beat the eggs lightly with the sugar in a 2 pint/1.1 litre bowl.

Remove the vanilla pod and pour the cream onto the eggs, whisking thoroughly all the time.

Strain this mixture into a buttered pie dish or souffle dish and sprinkle on the nutmeg. Stand the dish in a roasting tin containing enough hot water to come well up the side of the dish. Bake for 1 hour in a pre-heated oven 170°C/325°F/gas mark 3. Serve the custard hot or cold.

Gooseberry pie
Method

Choose a pie dish appropriate to the amount of gooseberries available. Top, tail and wash the gooseberries and pile them into the pie dish, which should be completely filled, even piled up slightly. Sprinkle the fruit liberally with sugar. A little water can be added to just cover the base of the pie dish. The fruit will produce enough juice as it cooks.

Make sufficient shortcrust pastry to cover the pie with a lid (there is no pastry base). Roll the pastry out on a floured surface to be ¼in/6mm thick. Dampen the rim of the pie dish with water then cut and press strips of pastry to line the rim. Dampen this strip so that the pastry lid can be attached to it. Make sure the remaining pastry is large enough to cover the pie without stretching. Carefully lift the pastry onto the fruit, pressing the edges to the strip on the rim of the pie dish.

To make sure there is a good seal use the prongs of a fork to press the pastries together. Trim off any excess pastry from around the edge of the pie but bear in mind that the pastry will shrink during cooking so do not trim too tightly.

Brush the surface of the pastry with milk or beaten egg and milk and make two slits in the top of the pie to let the steam out. Bake in a pre-heated oven 150°C/350°F/gas mark 4 for about 1 hour or until the pastry is golden brown.

Serve hot or cold with cream, custard or ice-cream.

Fair cakes

Fair cakes were especially made in the northern counties to be sold and eaten at the hiring fairs at Whitsun and Martinmas (11 November).

Whit cakes

Whit cakes are a variation of Eccles cakes (see the recipe on p. 80). The filling is slightly different as it has no sugar, but equal quantities of chopped candied peel and currants with a little lemon juice and mixed spice.

Curd cheesecakes

Cheesecakes, in one form or another, were one of the earliest sweet puddings. The Countess of Leicester's account book for 1265 shows that a considerable amount was spent on soft cheese for tarts. The cheese was pounded in a mortar with egg yolks, ginger, cinnamon and sugar to make the filling. This filling developed to include various concoctions made from curds, custard, butter and/or ground almonds. The best cheesecakes use sharp-tasting curd cheese. If this is not available cottage cheese can be used, but it will need to be sieved before use. The cheesecake recipes given here bear little resemblance to more modern packet versions, which often contain no cheese at all.

Basic cheesecake

Ingredients

9in/23cm flan tin lined with
   shortcrust pastry and baked blind
8oz/225g curd cheese
2oz/50g caster sugar
2 eggs, beaten
Grated rind of $\frac{1}{4}$ lemon
Juice of 1 lemon
2 tsp cornflour
2 tbsp double cream
1 tbsp butter, melted

Method

Blend the cheese with the sugar, beaten eggs, lemon rind and lemon juice. Beat well until the mixture is smooth, then add the cornflour mixed in the cream. Fold in the melted butter. Pour this mixture into the pastry case and bake in a pre-heated oven 190°C/375°F/gas mark 5 for 30 minutes. Serve the cheesecake cold.

Varying the basic cheesecake

Cooked or fresh fruit can be spread over the top of the finished cheesecake. To give a different texture 4oz/100g ground almonds can be added to the filling, with the addition of another egg. A further variation (and there are a few) eaten in Northamptonshire and Yorkshire is given below.

Ingredients

Curds from 1 pint/600ml of sour milk
1oz/25g margarine
$1\frac{1}{2}$oz/40g caster sugar
1 egg, well beaten
2oz/50g currants
$\frac{1}{4}$ tsp almond essence
Finely grated zest
   of 1 lemon
$\frac{1}{2}$ tsp grated nutmeg

Method

Put the margarine in a saucepan with the sugar and egg over a low heat and stir continuously until the mixture thickens, but is not curdled. Remove from heat and mix in the curds and the remaining ingredients. Allow to cool before pouring the mixture into the pastry case. Bake as for the basic cheesecake.

Trinity Sunday

This is the Sunday after Whitsun or the Day of Pentecost and was introduced into the Christian calendar in about AD 1000. It is the only time a doctrine of the Church is given a 'special' day. The Trinity – Father, Son and Holy Spirit – are the three facets of our God, a difficult concept to grapple with. The Trinity is especially important in Celtic Christianity, when prayers frequently include petitions to the three members separately, emphasizing the different attributes of Father, Son and Holy Spirit.

There is an interesting story about Eccles cakes, as a result of which I have made small Eccles cakes to give out to the congregation at the end of the Sunday service. I hoped the congregation would enjoy these at home, and also that the Eccles cakes would act as a reminder of Trinity Sunday.

Eccles comes from the word 'ecclesia', meaning church, and the town in Lancashire (not the one in Kent) used to be famous for these currant-filled pastry cakes especially made by local bakers to celebrate religious feast days. When the Puritans came to power they decided these more-ish little cakes were too rich and tasty. They thought Eccles cakes were probably pagan in origin, and in 1650 they passed a law which meant you could be sent to jail for eating an Eccles cake. I suppose the same fate also awaited you if you made them.

Happily that law has been repealed and you can enjoy an Eccles cake quite legally whenever you like – but especially on Trinity Sunday, as the three cuts which are always made on an Eccles cake represent Father, Son and Holy Spirit.

Ingredients

To make 16 cakes

8oz/225g puff pastry
Milk and caster sugar to glaze

For the filling

1oz/25g margarine
4oz/100g currants
2oz/50g mixed peel
1 level tbsp soft brown sugar
$1/_2$ tsp mixed spice

Eccles cakes
Method

To make the filling, melt the margarine in a saucepan and then stir in the other ingredients and leave the mixture to cool.

Roll out the pastry and cut out rounds with a $3^1/_2$in/8.5cm cutter. Place a heaped teaspoonful of filling in the centre of each pastry round, and dampen the edges of the rounds with milk or water. Gather the edges together and press together to give a good seal.

Turn the cakes over and place on a greased and floured or lined baking sheet so that the sealed edges are underneath. Now flatten each cake to a disc shape. Slash the top of each cake with three cuts (Father, Son and Holy Spirit), brush the tops with milk and sprinkle with caster sugar.

Bake in a pre-heated oven 210°C/425°F/gas mark 7 for 20-25 minutes or until golden brown. Cool on a wire rack.

Lammas

This celebration falls on 1 August, the feast day of St Peter in Chains, and marks the beginning of harvest. Lammas was originally a pagan festival which gradually developed into a Christian observance incorporating the Jewish Festival of First Fruits (Shavuot). The *Anglo-Saxon Chronicle* contains references to 'the feast of first fruits' which eventually evolved into Lammas, from the old English 'Hlafmaesse', meaning Loaf Mass.

The first corn to be cut from the new harvest was taken to the miller to grind, and a loaf of bread was made in time for the church service as a focus for the Lammas celebration. In some areas, such as the West Country, the bread was used during Holy Communion.

This custom was carried on until comparatively recently, especially in Scotland where a special Lammas Bannock was made (Bannock Lunastain).

This early Harvest Festival was marked by Lammas Fairs, at which a brittle toffee called Yellow Man was sold. The popular sweet was made in large blocks and chunks of toffee were broken off to sell. No doubt gingerbread biscuits, gingerbread and fairings were also available.

Bread recipes are to be found in the St Patrick and St David sections. See also the Harvest section, p. 84.

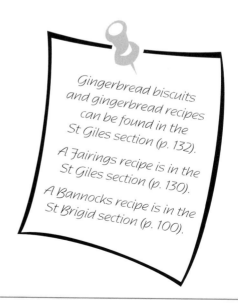

Gingerbread biscuits and gingerbread recipes can be found in the St Giles section (p. 132).

A Fairings recipe is in the St Giles section (p. 130).

A Bannocks recipe is in the St Brigid section (p. 100).

Ingredients

1oz/25g butter
8oz/225g brown
   sugar
1lb/450g golden
   syrup
1 dssp water
1 tsp vinegar
1 tsp bicarbonate
   of soda

Yellow man toffee
Method

Melt the butter in a medium to large saucepan, then add the sugar, golden syrup, water and vinegar.

Stir until all the ingredients are melted, then boil the mixture until it reaches the 'hard crack' stage (143°C/290°F).

To test this point, drop a little of the mixture into cold water, leave it for a moment, then pick it out between finger and thumb. When finger and thumb are separated a thread of toffee forms between them which should break sharply.

Now stir in the bicarbonate of soda and the mixture will foam up (at this stage it is like honeycomb. Pour the toffee into a well-greased tin, turning the edges with a spatula or palette knife.

When the toffee is cool enough to handle, pull it with well-buttered hands until it becomes pale in colour. When it is completely hardened break the Yellow man into rough pieces.

Shortbread

Ingredients

6oz/150g plain flour
4oz/100g hard margarine
   (although butter gives a
   better flavour)
2oz/50g caster sugar
A drop of vanilla essence
   (optional)

In Inverkeithing in Fife the Lammas Fair is still celebrated, the last of its ancient five fairs to survive. The Fair was begun in the twelfth century and over the years has undergone many changes; it is now celebrated on the second Wednesday of August. Along with the other goodies that were enjoyed at this time, shortbread was no doubt added to the list. There are many recipes but the one given below is a very simple, basic one.

Method

Rub the margarine or butter into the flour, stir in the sugar and work into a crumbly dough. Roll out on a lightly floured board, cut into desired shapes, and bake on a lined baking sheet. Alternatively, put the dough into a sandwich tin, marked into pieces. These will have to be re-cut once the shortbread is cooked. Prick the shortbread all over with a fork to prevent air bubbles from spoiling the finished biscuits. Bake in a pre-heated oven 160°C/320°F/gas mark 3 until the shortbread is a light golden brown.

Harvest

The Harvest celebration is one of the world's oldest festivals, pre-dating Christianity and celebrated by both the Ancient Greeks and the Romans. In Britain, as we have seen, the first cut of the corn was marked at Lammas; the cutting of the last sheaf at the end of the harvest was usually accompanied by the sacrifice of an animal, sometimes a hare. Gradually this was replaced by making a model of the animal out of straw instead, the origin of the 'corn dolly' which was hung in farmhouses until the following year. Before the traditional Harvest Festival church service, which was introduced only in the nineteenth century, farm workers and their families were given a celebratory meal, the 'harvest-home', as a thank you for all their hard work.

Today Harvest Festivals usually take place towards the end of September or early in October. Churches are decorated with flowers and greenery, fruit, vegetables and crops; many congregations now include tinned fruit in their displays, and the food is frequently given to the elderly or needy. Some churches still display the harvest loaf, baked in the shape of a sheaf of corn, in thankfulness for a good harvest. Harvest suppers are also enjoyed by many church communities early in the week after the Harvest Festival.

The Harvest Festival loaf

Before the potato was introduced to this country bread was the staple food. Wheat made the best and whitest bread which people preferred, but wheat only grows on well-fertilized soil so it was usually only the richer farmers and lords of the villages who had wheat bread. The bread eaten by poorer people was called maslin, and was made from a mixture of wheat and rye flour. Bread would have been used in place of plates, as 'trenchers', by the wealthy, and would have been thrown on the floor at the end of the meal to be eaten by the dogs. In the colder, wetter regions of the north and west bread flour was made from barley and oats. Weeds were often included with the grain and if the harvest was especially poor – or if the villagers were – beans, peas and even acorns would be ground to produce flour, and the bread produced was called horse bread. Whilst we may not want to eat horse bread today, there are many interesting bread flours available now that encourage the enjoyment and flavour of various grains and seeds.

Ingredients

3lb/1.5kg strong white flour
1 tbsp salt
1oz/25g fresh yeast
1 tsp sugar
2 50mg vitamin C tablets
1¹⁄₂ pints/900ml warm water
Beaten egg to glaze
Currants

Harvest Festival loaves

These can be used to decorate the church or a harvest supper venue.

Method

Sift the flour and salt into a large mixing bowl. Mix the fresh yeast with the sugar and crushed vitamin C tablets in the warm water. Add this to the flour and mix to give a firm dough. For large designs it is best to model the dough directly onto greased, upturned baking sheets. Use two sheets side by side on an oven rack so that the bread can be easily placed in the oven.

Loaves and fishes design

Divide the dough into halves. Use one half to roll out a large oval shape about 1in/2.5cm thick. Place this on the baking sheets. Use half of the remaining dough to form a very long 'sausage' which will go all round the edge of the oval. Twist this to form a rope and fix it in position with beaten egg. Make small flat fishes and tiny cottage loaves with the remaining dough and arrange these on the oval. Brush the whole arrangement with beaten egg and bake in a pre-heated oven 220°C/425°F/gas mark 7 for 20 minutes, then reduce the heat to 160°C/325°F/gas mark 3 and continue baking for a further 30 minutes or until golden brown.

Wheatsheaf design

Measure 8oz/225g dough and form it into a 'sausage' shape 12in/30cm long. Place this in the centre of the baking sheets and flatten it slightly, to form the base of the design. Take 12oz/350g dough and form a crescent shape. Arrange this at the top end of the 'sausage' and flatten it slightly. This will form the base for the top of the wheatsheaf. Use half the remaining dough to make thin 'sausages' about the thickness of a pencil and 12in/30cm long. Arrange these on the basic stalk part of the design, being sure to cover the base completely. Use three similar strands to plait together and lay across the stalks like string, tucking the ends under. Use 2oz/50g dough to make a little mouse to sit on the stalks. Use currants for its eyes. Divide the remaining dough into 1oz/25g pieces. Form these into little 'sausages' and arrange these all over the crescent shape like sun rays. Clip each 'sausage' shape two or three times with scissors to make 'V' shapes – these are the ears of corn. Brush over the entire design with beaten egg. Bake as for the loaves and fishes version.

These designs are not usually eaten and will keep for years if coated with artists' varnish.

Cold brisket of beef in cider

Ingredients

To serve 6-8 people

3-4lb/1.4-1.8kg salted brisket
  of beef, soaked overnight in
  cold water and drained
2 carrots, peeled and cut into
  thick slices
1 onion, peeled and quartered
Salt and pepper
A bundle of fresh mixed herbs
  – parsley, thyme, sage and
  marjoram
12 peppercorns
12 cloves
1 tsp allspice
1 tsp ground mace
1 pint/575-600ml cider
1 pint/575-600ml boiling water

Cider was widely drunk in Britain before fresh water
was readily available, and when there was no tea,
coffee or chocolate. The West Country produced the
largest volumes of cider. Cooking with cider naturally
followed, and this dish, served cold with salad,
pickles, and homemade bread was traditional fare at
harvest-homes.

Method

Put the beef in a large casserole with the carrot and
onion. Season with salt and pepper. Add the herbs and
spices. Pour on the cider and boiling water. Cover tightly
and cook in a pre-heated oven 130°C/250°F/gas mark $\frac{1}{2}$
for 4 hours.

Remove from the oven and allow the meat to cool in the
liquid overnight. The next morning remove the meat and
put it in a deep basin. Cover the meat with a plate that
fits under the rim of the basin and put a heavy weight on
the plate. Leave this in a cool place until the next day.
Serve the meat cut in thin slices.

Ox tongue
This is a medieval delicacy of offal that
was considered fit for gentlemen. At
first tongues were roasted, then later
they were chopped and pressed and
more lately pickled; they were an
essential part of a harvest supper
celebration spread. Now tongues can
be bought from good butchers or sliced
from delicatessen shops or counters.

Bacon and egg flan

Ingredients

To serve 4 people

7in/18cm flan ring or tin lined
    with shortcrust pastry
6oz/175g lean, green bacon
    rashers, rinds cut off
2 eggs
Salt and pepper
1/4 pint/150ml creamy milk or
    single cream

This was probably eaten out in the fields during the harvesting but it makes a tasty addition to a celebration harvest supper. The bacon would have been served as a chunk with an onion and bread to be eaten at midday. Alternatively, an egg and bacon flan would have been large enough for the whole family to eat when all were involved in the harvest.

Method

Cut 4oz/100g bacon rashers into strips about 2in/5cm long and line the pastry case with them.

Cut the remaining bacon rashers finely and scatter them over the bacon strips. Beat the eggs together and season generously, then beat in the milk or cream and pour this mixture over the bacon.

Bake in the centre of a pre-heated oven 190°C/375°F/gas mark 5 for 30 minutes or until the filling is golden brown. If liked, a little grated cheese can be sprinkled over the flan before baking. Serve the flan hot or cold with salad.

Fidget pie

Ingredients

To serve 4 people

1lb/450g potatoes, peeled and
 sliced
12oz/350g gammon, rind and
 fat removed, and diced
2 large onions, peeled and
 sliced
3 large cooking apples,
 peeled, cored and thinly
 sliced
2 tsp sugar
$1/2$ tsp dried thyme
Salt and pepper
$1/2$ pint/300ml stock
8oz/225g shortcrust pastry

The name of this pie derives from the fact that it used to be 'fitched' or five-sided in shape. It was a very popular dish at harvest time. If times were hard the pie would be made of vegetables only; in better times gammon was used. When the pie was made as a special treat the amount of gammon was halved and lamb chops, from the scrag end of neck, were put in – one for each person.

Method

Put a layer of sliced potatoes in the bottom of a 2 pint/1.1 litre pie dish. Cover this with a layer of gammon, a layer of onions and a layer of apples. Sprinkle with sugar.

Repeat these layers until the dish is full, finishing with a gammon layer. Sprinkle with dried thyme and season. Pour in sufficient stock to just cover the pie filling. Roll out the pastry to $1/4$in/5mm thick.

Cut strips of pastry to put on the dampened rim of the pie dish, then dampen these and lay the pastry lid over the pie.

Seal the edges by pressing down with the prongs of a fork or handle of a spoon. Make two slits in the pie lid.

Brush with milk or beaten egg and milk. Bake in a pre-heated oven 200°C/400°F/gas mark 6, at the top of the oven for about 20 minutes, then on a lower shelf for a further 55 minutes. Cover the pie with foil or brown paper if the pastry is browning too much.

If chops are to be added to the pie, lay them on top of the first layer of potatoes.

Harvest pudding

Ingredients

6-8 medium thickness slices of
    bread and butter
1lb/400g cooking apples,
    peeled, cored and sliced
2oz/50g shredded suet
3oz/75g soft brown sugar
2oz/50g raisins
Grated rind of 1 lemon
2 eggs
$^1/_2$ pint/250ml milk

This is a simple pudding to make and is a variation on the ever-popular Summer pudding.

Method

Line a pie dish with some of the bread and butter, with the butter on the outside. Mix together the apples, suet, sugar, raisins and lemon rind and fill the pie dish with this mixture.

Cover with more of the bread and butter with the butter side uppermost. Beat the eggs and milk together and pour over the top of the pudding. Cover and put the pudding in a cool place for about 2 hours. Bake in a pre-heated oven 170°C/350°F/gas mark 4 for about 1 hour. Serve this pudding warm with cream.

Ingredients

6oz/175g butter
4oz/100g caster sugar
3 eggs, beaten
8oz/225g self-raising flour,
    white or wholemeal
6oz/175g sultanas
1oz/25g walnuts, chopped
Finely grated rind of 1 orange
3-4 tbsp orange juice

Golden harvest cake

A simple, inexpensive fruit cake.

Method

Cream butter and sugar together until light and fluffy. Beat in the eggs and sifted flour alternately a little at a time. Stir in the sultanas, walnuts and orange rind and sufficient orange juice to give the mixture a soft, dropping consistency.

Put into a greased and lined 7in/18cm cake tin and bake in a pre-heated oven 170°C/325°F/gas mark 3 for $1^1/_4$-$1^1/_2$ hours or until the cake is golden brown and firm to the touch. Leave in the tin for about 10 minutes, then turn it out to complete cooling on a wire rack.

All Saints' and All Souls'

All Saints' Day falls on 1 November, followed by All Souls' on 2 November. All Saints' Day was a holiday in Britain until the Reformation and still is in some parts of Europe. All Saints' and All Souls' is not just a time for remembering the saints, but is a season of remembrance for all who have died, especially our loved ones and our memories of them. In pre-Christian times there was a belief that the souls of the dead returned at this time to eat normal food, and in some areas wine and 'soul cakes' were placed on people's graves.

Eventually the custom was changed into 'souling' or 'soul-caking' when children went from house to house singing songs and receiving gifts of cake, sweets or money. The cakes, which were given away to all visitors, varied from small fruit cakes, caraway seed cakes, or a light flat bun, spiced and sweetened, to small loaves of bread made with wheat or barley flour. It was felt that by giving cakes away one was somehow helping the souls in Purgatory, by reducing the amount of time they spent there.

Today these customs have been absorbed into the commercial Hallowe'en and into the custom of 'trick or treat', which is American in origin.

Colcannon

Ingredients

To serve 4-6 people

1lb/450g cabbage or kale,
    washed and shredded
1lb/450g potatoes, peeled and
    cut into pieces
2 leeks, washed, trimmed and
    chopped
¼ pint/125ml creamy milk or
    single cream
4oz/100g butter, melted
Salt and pepper
1 pinch mace

This is a traditional Hallowe'en recipe and often contained charms: a ring for marriage, a horseshoe or coin for luck. There are local variations in the ingredients and originally Colcannon was made with kale, but now it is more usually made with cabbage.

Method

Boil the potatoes and cabbage or kale in separate saucepans until they are cooked. Simmer the chopped leeks in the milk for 5-10 minutes.

Drain the potatoes and cabbage very well. Mash the potatoes, stir in the leeks and the milk, the cabbage, seasoning and mace.

Mix well, tip into a serving dish and reheat in the oven. Make a well in the centre of the colcannon just before serving and pour in the melted butter. Serve each portion with a spoonful of butter.

Gingerbread

Gingerbread biscuits, cut out with an angel cutter and wrapped in silver or gold foil, are an appropriate little gift for people who attend church services on All Saints' or All Souls' Days. See recipes in St Giles section, p. 130

Boxty pancakes

Ingredients

To serve 4 people

1lb/450g potatoes, peeled
4oz/100g self-raising flour
3-4fl oz/90-125 ml milk
Sea salt and freshly ground
    black pepper
2oz/50g bacon fat or butter

Boxty pancakes were traditionally eaten on All Hallows Eve, especially in northern counties of England and Ireland. Pancakes are usually made from flour, eggs and milk, but these are made mainly from potatoes, with some flour and milk. Frying them in bacon fat gives them extra flavour, but of course makes them no longer a vegetarian dish.

Method

Grate the potatoes and put them in a colander, cover with kitchen towels and press down to squeeze out the surplus starch. Sift the flour into a bowl, stir in the milk followed by the potatoes and season with salt and pepper. Heat the fat in a frying pan and once it stops foaming drop in about 1 tablespoon of batter to make each boxty.

Cook the pancakes for 3-4 minutes or until they are golden brown on each side. Remove from the pan and keep them warm under a moderate grill until all the pancakes have been cooked. Sprinkle with salt and serve.

As a variation the pancakes can be flavoured with caraway seeds, sage or chopped onions. Some recipes also suggest that half the potatoes are boiled and mashed before adding to the rest of the ingredients, with a small egg beaten into the mixture.

Buttermilk can be used in place of the milk (and egg, if used) and then the pancakes can be eaten sprinkled with sugar.

All Souls' Day almond biscuits

Ingredients

To make 24-30 biscuits

3oz/75g plain flour
Grated zest of 1 lemon
5oz/125g ground almonds
4oz/100g caster sugar
1 tbsp brandy (or milk)
$^1/_2$oz/15g butter
1 egg, beaten
12-15 blanched almonds,
    split to give 24 -30 pieces

These biscuits are chewy and moist and are traditionally eaten on All Souls' Day, but they will keep for a week.

Method

Sift the flour into a mixing bowl and add the lemon zest, ground almonds, sugar and mix. Add the brandy (or milk), butter and the beaten egg until the mixture holds together and does not stick to the bowl.

With damp hands roll pieces of the dough to form 1in/2.5cm balls and place them, spaced, on greased or lined baking sheets. Press half an almond into the middle of each biscuit.

Bake in a pre-heated oven 180°C/360°F/gas mark 4 for 15-20 minutes. Allow the biscuits to cool on the baking sheet for 5 minutes before putting them on a wire rack.

Soul cakes

Ingredients

2 sticks of butter (4oz/100g)
$3^3/_4$ cups flour
1 cup caster sugar
$^1/_4$ tsp nutmeg or mace
1 tsp each cinnamon, ginger,
  mixed spice
2 eggs
2 tsp malt or cider vinegar

These cakes were made especially in the Midlands and northern counties of England. Various traditions are linked to them, but unfortunately they are not made any more. Why not revive this tradition and bake them for children to take out with them and instead of 'trick or treating' give the householder a cake? Or you could make some soul cakes yourself to give to the children when they call.

Method

Rub the butter into the sifted flour, and stir in the sugar and spices. Mix into a stiff dough with the beaten eggs and vinegar. Knead the dough, then roll out to $^1/_4$in/5mm thick and cut into 3in/8cm rounds. Arrange the cakes on a greased or lined baking sheet, prick them with a fork and bake them in a pre-heated oven 180°C/350°F/gas mark 4 until golden brown. While still warm sprinkle the cakes with icing sugar.

Alternatively the butter and sugar may be creamed together, the beaten eggs and vinegar worked in and the flour and spices mixed in to make a stiff dough. Knead and roll out as above.

Ingredients

To serve 6 people

4lb/1.8kg chicken
1/4 pint/150ml malt vinegar
2 tbsp soft brown sugar

For the stuffing

1lb/450g prunes, soaked , or
    'ready to eat'
2oz/50g almonds, blanched
    and chopped
8oz/225g fresh, white
    breadcrumbs
1 tsp each of chopped fresh
    sage, parsley, marjoram and
    thyme or 2 tsp mixed dried
    herbs
2oz/50g shredded suet
1-2 tbsp vinegar
Salt and pepper

Lemon Sauce

1oz/25g butter
1oz/25g plain flour
3/4 pint/450ml chicken stock
2 eggs, beaten
Grated rind and juice of 2
    lemons
Garnish
Parsley sprigs and lemon slices

Hendle Wakes
Method

To make the stuffing: As necessary, drain and stone the prunes, set six aside and chop the rest. Mix together the prunes, almonds, breadcrumbs, herbs, suet and vinegar. Season well.

Wash the chicken and remove giblets. Spoon the stuffing into the neck cavity and secure the cavity so that the stuffing does not come out during cooking. Put the chicken in a large, heavy-based saucepan and cover the chicken with cold water, add the vinegar and sugar. Bring to the boil and then reduce to a simmer. Put a lid on the saucepan and cook for about 4 hrs or until the bird is tender. Remove from the heat and leave the chicken in the stock until the next morning. Remove the chicken, skin it and put it on a large serving dish. Strain 3/4 pint/450ml of the stock from the saucepan into a smaller saucepan and heat it through.

To make the lemon sauce: Melt the butter in a small saucepan, sift in the flour and cook for a minute or two before adding the warmed chicken stock. Continue to cook gently until the sauce is smooth and creamy. Mix a couple of tablespoons of this into the beaten eggs, strain this into the sauce. Heat the sauce gently until it thickens, stir all the time and do not let the sauce boil or curdle. Remove from the heat, blend in the lemon juice and half the lemon rind and season. Set aside to cool. Coat the chicken with the sauce, sprinkle over the remaining lemon rind. Cut the prunes, set aside earlier, into halves to give 12 pieces and use these to decorate the chicken. Complete the decoration with sprigs of parsley and slices of lemon.

Soup can be made from the remaining stock and lemon sauce heated together and a swirl of cream added before serving.

St Kentigern
14 January

Though there is little known about Kentigern, he is said to have been a native of Lothian, and he may have been a founder of the church at Glasgow, and a missionary to Cumbria. He was born in Culross after his mother was cast aside by her father when she revealed that she was pregnant. The young Kentigern was then raised by a hermit who nicknamed him 'Mungo' meaning 'most dear'. He became a Celtic monk and evangelist in the Strathclyde area, but persecution against Christians drove him into Wales, where it is said he founded the monastery at Llanelwy, before travelling north to Dumfries and Glasgow. Legend has it that he met with Columba shortly before Columba died, and exchanged pastoral staffs with him. Kentigern is the patron saint of Glasgow, and his shrine is in St Mungo's Cathedral there. The ring and the fish on the arms of the city refer to a legend that Kentigern saved an unfaithful wife from the anger of her husband by finding her missing ring inside a salmon. So it seems appropriate to celebrate the saint's feast day with salmon recipes.

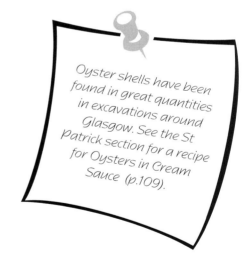

Oyster shells have been found in great quantities in excavations around Glasgow. See the St Patrick section for a recipe for Oysters in Cream Sauce (p.109).

Salmon in pastry

Ingredients

To serve 6 people

2 thick salmon fillets about
    2$\frac{1}{2}$lb/1.1 kg, skinned and
    boned
3oz/75g butter
2 pieces of ginger in syrup
1 tbsp currants
Salt and pepper
8oz/225g shortcrust pastry
1 egg, beaten, to glaze

Cooking salmon in pastry is the medieval equivalent of cooking in foil, but it has the advantage of adding substance to the meal as well as sealing in the essential oils, juices and flavours from the salmon.

Method

Season the salmon fillets with salt and pepper.

Mash the butter, then chop the ginger and work this into the butter. Add the currants to this mixture, then sandwich two-thirds of it between the salmon fillets and spread the rest of the butter mixture on top.

Roll out the pastry to about $\frac{1}{4}$in/5mm thick, then carefully lift the fish into the centre of the pastry and enclose it, firmly sealing the pastry round it. Trim away any surplus pastry and carefully lift the salmon parcel onto a greased baking sheet, inverting it so that the central 'seam' in the pastry is now underneath.

Slash the top of the pastry case in three places to allow the steam to escape. Use the pastry trimmings to cut out decorative shapes to fix to the top of the parcel, and then brush the top with beaten egg. Bake in a pre-heated oven 220°C/425°F/gas mark 7 for 30 minutes or until golden brown.

This can be served with a rich cream and mixed herb sauce and seasonal vegetables.

Ingredients

To make a useful amount

8oz/225g plain flour
4oz/100g margarine
About 2 tbsp cold water

Shortcrust Pastry
Method

This pastry is made with 1 part fat to 2 parts flour. You can use half margarine and half lard, but many people now prefer to use all margarine. Pastry is best made with cold hands in cool surroundings. Rub the fat into the flour to give a breadcrumb texture. (If a food processor or food mixer is used the rubbing-in stage is quicker.)

Add enough cold water to bind the 'crumbs' into a soft, but not sticky, dough. The amount of water varies depending on the flour used and the consistency is best judged if this stage is done by hand, even if you have used a processor for the rubbing-in. The pastry is best left to rest in a cool place for about 15 minutes before being placed on a floured surface to be rolled out. A light touch is essential when making and handling pastry; repeated handling and rolling out will make the end result heavy.

Salmon with fennel sauce

Ingredients

To serve 4 people

4 x 6oz/175g salmon steaks
2 shallots, peeled and finely
    chopped
1 small fennel bulb, finely
    chopped
1 bay leaf
2 stalks parsley, crushed
$1/4$ pint/150ml dry white wine
4oz/100g butter

For the sauce

2 egg yolks, beaten together
Salt and pepper
A little lemon juice
Sprigs of fresh fennel, to
    garnish

A simple dish made special by the addition of a tasty sauce.

Method

Place the salmon steaks in an ovenproof dish, and scatter the shallots, fennel, parsley and bay leaf over the top. Pour on the wine and cover the dish with a lid or foil. Bake in a pre-heated oven for 15 minutes at 180°C/350°F/gas mark 4, or until the steaks are tender.

Strain off 4fl oz/100ml of the cooking liquid. Turn off the oven, cover the salmon and replace in the oven to keep warm.

Boil the strained liquid until it has reduced to about 1 tablespoonful. Put the egg yolks in a heatproof bowl, stir in the reduced liquid and half the butter. Place the bowl over a saucepan of boiling water and whisk until the butter has melted, then slowly whisk in the remaining butter and carry on whisking to make a thick fluffy sauce.

Take the bowl from the saucepan and stir in 2 tsp of the cooked fennel, season the sauce to taste and add a little lemon juice, if liked. Transfer the salmon to warm plates and spoon over the sauce. Serve with seasonal vegetables.

St Brigid
1 February

There are few historical facts about St Brigid, also known as St Bride, and some authorities doubt that she existed at all. In Ireland, however, she ranks in importance second only to St Patrick. She is thought to have been born to humble parents living about five miles from the abbey at Kildare. She became a nun at an early age, and eventually became abbess of the double monastery there. Although little is known about her she seems to have been a happy, caring and compassionate person – known for healing the sick, blessing the poor and singing to her cows so that they produced above-average yields of milk. Her emblem includes a flame as she is associated with the Holy Spirit, and after her death the nuns of Kildare kept a perpetual fire burning in the abbey for centuries in her memory. She was buried in Kildare, but when the abbey was invaded by the Danes her remains were moved to Downpatrick, where they are said to have been buried with those of St Patrick.

Brigid's veneration spread throughout Ireland and into Europe. Some 19 churches are dedicated to her in England, the most well known being St Bride's in Fleet Street, the 'journalists' church'. The Irish celebrate her feast day with Barm brack (an Irish tea bread), and the Scots bake the special St Bride's Bannock.

The recipes that follow are for Barm brack, Bannocks and Bara brith (which means 'speckled bread'). All these tea breads can be enjoyed plain, buttered or toasted.

Ingredients

7fl oz/200ml tea made with
   1$\frac{1}{2}$ tbsp tea leaves
6oz/160g soft brown sugar
3fl oz/75ml Irish whiskey
6oz/160g sultanas
6oz/160g raisins
6oz/160g plain flour
1$\frac{1}{2}$ tsp baking powder
1 tsp mixed spice
1 pinch salt
1 egg, beaten

Ingredients

12oz/340g plain flour
1 tsp bicarbonate of soda
1 tsp cream of tartar
1oz/25g caster sugar
4oz/100g sultanas
$\frac{1}{2}$ pint/250ml buttermilk
   or sour milk
Caster sugar for dredging

Ingredients

$\frac{3}{4}$ pint/375ml tea
12oz/325g mixed dried fruit
1lb/450g self-raising flour
1 tsp mixed spice
1 egg

Barm brack
Method

Brew the tea, strain it and whilst still warm add the sugar and stir until dissolved. Add the whiskey and the fruit, and allow the fruit to soak in the tea for 30-60 minutes.

Sift the dry ingredients into a bowl, make a well in the centre and pour in the beaten egg and the tea infusion and fruit. Mix well to make a thick batter, spoon this into a lined 8in/20cm loaf tin and bake on the centre shelf of a pre-heated oven 150°C/300°F/gas mark 2 for 1$\frac{1}{2}$ hours. Turn out onto a rack to cool.

Bannocks
Method

Sift the flour, bicarbonate of soda and cream of tartar into a bowl, stir in the sugar and fruit, add the milk and mix to form a soft dough. Place this in a well-greased 7in/18cm sandwich tin and spread evenly in the tin. Bake for 30 minutes in a pre-heated oven 200°C/400°F/gas mark 6.

Remove the bannock from the tin and sprinkle the surface with a little extra caster sugar. Keep the surface of the bannock soft by wrapping it in a clean tea towel and cool on a wire rack.

Bara brith
Method

To make this traditional Welsh fruit bread, soak the dried fruit in the tea overnight. Sift the flour and spice into a mixing bowl, stir in the beaten egg, the tea and the fruit and mix well. Spoon the mixture into a lined loaf tin and bake in a pre-heated oven 150°C/300°F/gas mark 2 for 1$\frac{1}{2}$ hours. Remove from the tin and cool on a wire rack.

St David
1 March

According to legend and the writings of his tenth-century biographer, Rhugyfarch, the patron saint of Wales was the son of a Cardigan chieftain, who studied under St Paulinus, founded 12 monasteries, and went on pilgrimage to Jerusalem, where he was consecrated bishop by the patriarch of that city. Few of these facts are probably correct. David may have been born at Henfynw in Cardigan, and founded the monastery of Menevia (modern-day St David's in Pembrokeshire). He modelled the monastery on those of the Desert Fathers in Egypt, and it was an extremely strict regime. The monks lived on a diet of bread and vegetables, and drank mainly water – David was traditionally known as 'the Waterman', indicating that he and the monks were probably teetotal.

There are over 50 churches dedicated to David in south Wales, and others in Devon, Cornwall and Brittany. Several Irish saints are said to have visited Menevia to be David's pupils, so that he can be said to have influenced Irish monasticism. The traditional wearing of daffodils and eating leeks on St David's Day have never been explained satisfactorily, but as both are still observed, I have included two recipes containing leeks, and as David's monks ate mostly bread and vegetables, there are also recipes for bread and for a vegetarian version of shepherd's pie.

Ingredients

To serve 4-6 people

1¼lb/575g leeks, washed and trimmed
2 large onions, peeled and finely chopped
3 sticks celery with leaves, washed and chopped

1 large potato, peeled and chopped
1 tbsp chopped parsley
2oz/50g butter
2½ pints/1.4 litres white or chicken stock
Salt and pepper
¼ pint/150ml double cream

Cream of leek soup
Method

Put a small leek to one side, and roughly chop the rest. Melt the butter in a large, heavy-based saucepan and add the chopped leeks, onion and celery and cook over a low heat for 10-15 minutes, until the vegetables are soft and transparent.

Add the potato and continue to cook over a low heat as the butter is absorbed. Add the parsley and slowly pour in the stock. Season with salt and pepper and bring the soup to the boil. Put a lid on the saucepan and simmer the soup for about 30 minutes. Liquidize the soup after it has cooled a little. Return the soup to a clean saucepan, stir in the cream and reheat, then stir in the sliced raw leek just prior to serving.

Simple leek soup
If you want to make a simple, quick leek soup, simmer some washed chopped leeks in good stock, and when they are soft cool the soup, liquidize and season to taste. Reheat before serving.

Basic white bread
Ingredients

1¹/₂lb/700g strong white flour
1oz/25g margarine or lard
2 tsp salt
2 tsp sugar
1 oz/25g fresh yeast
1 50mg vitamin C tablet, crushed
³/₄ pint/375ml warm water

Method

Sift the flour into a large mixing bowl and rub in the fat, then stir in the salt and sugar. The crushed vitamin C tablet can be added too, or it can be dissolved in the warm water together with the yeast. Add the liquid to the flour mixture and stir to make a dough. Knead for 2-3 minutes in a food mixer.
Turn out the dough onto a lightly floured board and knead until the dough is smooth. Mould into the required loaf shape, such as a plait, or a circular loaf, or put it into greased loaf tins; otherwise divide the dough into equally sized rolls and place on greased baking sheets. Dust the top of the dough with flour, and put it in a warm place to rise. The bread should be at least twice the original size before it is put in a pre-heated oven 200°C/400°F/gas mark 6 to bake until the bread sounds hollow when the lower surface is tapped. Timing will depend on the size and shape of the loaves or rolls. Approximate times are as follows:
Rolls: 15-20 minutes; 1lb/450g loaf: 35 minutes; 2lb/900g loaf: 50 minutes.

Wholemeal bread

The recipe given below can be adapted to your personal taste; some people find bread made from all wholemeal flour too heavy and solid. Using equal proportions of white and wholemeal flour gives a lighter loaf.

Ingredients

1¹/₂lb/700g wholemeal flour
2oz/50g margarine
2 tsp salt
2 tsp sugar
1oz/25g fresh yeast
1 50mg vitamin C tablet
³/₄ pint/375ml warm water

Method

As for white bread.

Soda bread does not use yeast, and a recipe for it is found in the St Patrick's section on p. 107.

Ingredients

4oz/100g aduki beans
2oz/50g wheat grain or rice
2 pints/1.1 litres water for
  boiling
1 tbsp oil
1 onion, peeled and finely
  chopped
8oz/225g carrots, peeled and
  finely chopped
1-2 tbsp soy sauce
2 tbsp tomato purée
1 tsp mixed herbs
$\frac{1}{2}$ pint/275ml aduki bean stock
Salt and pepper
1lb/450g potatoes, peeled
1oz/25g butter

Vegetarian shepherd's pie
Method

Wash the aduki beans and with the wheat grain or rice soak in water overnight, or steep them in boiling water for 1 hour. Drain and rinse, then bring them to the boil in fresh water and cook for 50 minutes or until the wheat grain or rice is fairly soft. Drain, reserving the stock. Heat the oil in a saucepan and fry the onion for 5 minutes, add the carrots and cook for 2-3 minutes, then add the beans and grains.

Mix the soy sauce, tomato purée and herbs with the stock, pour this over the beans and vegetable mixture, bring to the boil and simmer for 20-30 minutes. Season to taste. Add a little more liquid if necessary so that the final mixture is moist. Transfer to a greased 3 pint/1.5 litre casserole.

Boil the potatoes until soft and mash them with the butter, season well and spread over the beans and vegetables. Bake for 35-40 minutes at 180°C/350°F/gas mark 4, until the potato is crisp and brown.

St Patrick
17 March

Patrick was born somewhere on the west coast between the Clyde and the Severn. His father Calpurnius was a civil official and a deacon; his grandfather was a priest. When Patrick was 16 he was kidnapped by Irish raiders and taken to Ireland, where he worked as a herdsman in Antrim. During this time, committing himself to regular prayer, he began to think seriously about religion, laying the foundations for his future missions. After six years he escaped to the Continent, and trained for the priesthood. In a dream he felt called to return to preach the gospel to his former captors, and he returned to Armagh with a small group of followers. It was Patrick who helped to establish the gospel in Ireland and brought the Irish Church into existence. A famous story recounts Patrick's confrontation, at Tara in Meath, with the high king Laoghaire on Easter Eve, when Patrick kindled the paschal light on the hill of Slane, silencing the druids and establishing himself as a preacher of faith and power.

Patrick became the most important figure of Christian mission in Ireland, and his influence was far-reaching. A few years after his death the Irish missionary Columba left to take his mission to Iona, and from there the gospel message spread through Scotland and into Northumberland.

Traditionally St Patrick's Day food should include fish, as a story relates that Patrick was offered some meat during Lent and he threw it into the sea in disgust as meat would certainly not have been on his Lenten menu. The meat is said to have turned into a fish – which would have been more acceptable. Nowadays, St Patrick's Day celebrations are more likely to feature potato soup, boiled bacon and cabbage – all washed down with stout, porter or whiskey.

Potato soup

Ingredients

To serve 4-6 people

2 rashers streaky bacon, rinds
    removed and chopped
1oz/25g butter
1½lb/700g potatoes, after
    they have been peeled and
    chopped
2 onions, peeled and chopped
1½ pints/850ml chicken stock
½ pint/280ml milk
6 sprigs parsley, tied together
Salt and white pepper
¼ pint/140ml single cream

Garnish

1 rasher streaky bacon
Freshly chopped parsely

This is a good, wholesome, traditional Irish soup incorporating two ingredients which are readily available – bacon and potatoes.

Method

Fry the bacon in a saucepan until the fat starts to run, then add the butter, potatoes and onions and continue to cook, stirring all the time. Add the stock, milk and parsley sprigs and seasoning. Bring the mixture to the boil, put the lid on the saucepan and simmer for 30-40 minutes.

Allow the soup to cool slightly, remove the parsley sprigs and purée the soup in a liquidizer. Return the soup to a clean saucepan and stir in the cream, then reheat the soup without allowing it to boil.

To finish the dish, cut the rind off the streaky bacon, then chop and fry it until crisp. Serve the soup in bowls, garnished with the crispy bacon and chopped parsley.

For a vegetarian version just omit the bacon and substitute vegetable stock for the chicken stock, adding an onion.

Traditional soda bread

Ingredients

1lb/450g wholemeal flour
8oz/225g white flour
1 tsp salt
1 tsp bicarbonate of soda
$1/_2$ pint/280ml buttermilk
1oz/25g rolled oats, optional
Beaten egg to glaze, if liked

The enjoyment of potato soup is enhanced if eaten with traditional soda bread. This is also known as soda cake, because the loaves are traditionally round. The bread should be made and eaten on the same day as it does not keep. The 'everyday' loaf is made with mainly wholemeal flour, but for special occasions white is used.

Method

Mix the flours, salt, bicarbonate of soda and rolled oats, if using, in a bowl and add sufficient buttermilk to bind the ingredients into a soft dough. Turn the dough out onto a lightly floured surface, knead very lightly and shape into a round loaf. Place the loaf on a greased baking sheet and using a sharp knife cut a cross on the top of the loaf.

This cross on the soda bread, and also on hot cross buns, was a tradition in pre-Reformation days when all bread was marked with a cross as a charm against evil spirits that might stop the bread from rising. An alternative view is that the quadrants formed by the cross represent the four seasons.

Glaze the top of the loaf with beaten egg if liked. Bake in a pre-heated oven 200°C/400°F/gas mark 6 for 20-30 minutes or until the bread sounds hollow when tapped on the base.

The bread is best served in warm, buttered slices.

Boiled bacon

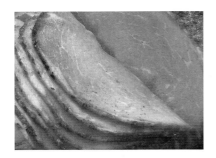

Pork was the most readily available meat for British farm workers for many centuries. Pigs were cheap to feed as they would forage for themselves and would also eat household scraps and leftovers. After the pigs were slaughtered the meat needed less salting than other meats and it stayed juicier for longer, which was an important consideration as one pig might well have to feed a family for six months. The meat could also be smoked to produce cured hams and sides of bacon.

The size, leanness and cost of a bacon joint varies according to individual taste. Gammon is the leanest joint but is more expensive than collar and forehock. Some recipes suggest pre-soaking and various additions to the cooking water, but some of the best ham I have tasted was cooked by a chef who simply soaked the bacon joint in water with nothing added. Cooking time is 20 minutes per lb/450g of meat plus 20 minutes.

If eaten hot, ham is often served with parsley sauce.

Parsley sauce
Ingredients

1/2oz/15g butter
1/2oz/15g plain flour
1/2 pint/300ml milk
2 tbsp chopped fresh parsley
Salt and pepper

Method

Put the butter, flour and milk in a saucepan, and heat and whisk continuously until the sauce thickens, boils and is smooth. Season and stir in the chopped parsley.

Oysters in cream sauce

Ingredients

To serve 4 people

2 dozen oysters
1oz/25g butter
1oz/25g flour
$1/2$ pint/125ml milk
1 tbsp dry sherry
2 tbsp double cream
$1/2$ tsp salt
A pinch of cayenne pepper
4 slices hot buttered toast
Paprika

Oysters are another favourite dish for St Patrick's Day. They are in season from September to April, and, if ready to be eaten, their shells should first be tight, closed and intact. To prepare the oysters scrub all grit from the closed shells using a stiff brush. Then hold the shell on a flat surface with one hand and insert the point of a short, strong knife in the crack between the shells near the hinge. Ease the knife in order to cut the muscle holding the oyster to the flat, upper shell, and at the same time twist the knife to prise open the shell, always keeping the flat shell on the top. Remove the flat shell to show the oyster and the juices in the deeper bottom shell. As a safety precaution hold the oyster in a clean tea towel in case the knife slips.

Method

Open the oysters and reserve the liquor. Melt the butter in a saucepan and stir in the flour, cook gently for a minute, then gradually blend in the oyster liquor and milk. Cook the sauce until it comes to the boil and thickens. Add the sherry, cream and oysters and season to taste with salt and cayenne pepper, then simmer for a further 4 minutes. Spoon the sauce and oysters onto hot buttered toast and sprinkle with paprika.

Oatcakes

Ingredients

8oz/225g plain flour
1 tsp salt
1lb/450g medium oatmeal
4oz/100g melted margarine
1 tbsp sugar, preferably
   'caster'
1 tsp bicarbonate of soda
5 tbsp warm water

Whilst very good oatcakes can be bought in supermarkets, it is sometimes nice to make your own and they will, of course, have a better flavour.

Method

Sift the flour, salt and bicarbonate of soda in a mixing bowl, add the sugar and oatmeal and mix together. Bind the dry ingredients together using the melted margarine and the water. Tip out the dough onto a floured surface and roll out to a thickness of about $1/8$in/2.5mm and cut into rounds 2in/5cm in diametre. Place the oatcakes on greased baking sheets and bake in a pre-heated oven 190°C/ 375°F/gas mark 5 for 20 minutes. Cool on a wire rack.

St Mark
25 April

The author of the second Gospel; the companion of Peter and Paul on missionary journeys; the John Mark mentioned in Acts; and the young man who ran away without his robe when Jesus was arrested in Gethsemane – all are identified as St Mark. Mark went with Paul and Barnabas on their first mission but turned back after a rift with Paul, who then refused to take Mark with him on his later journey. Mark instead joined Barnabas to continue their mission to Cyprus. Later the breach with Paul was healed, since Mark is recorded as working with Paul in Rome, where he also wrote his Gospel, some say at the dictation of Peter. After Paul and Peter's death Mark probably went to Egypt; traditionally he was the first bishop of the Church there and was martyred, though the truth of this is uncertain. His shrine in Alexandria nevertheless became a place of pilgrimage. His relics were taken from there to Venice in the ninth century where they remain under the basilica of St Mark's, and where there are also some fine mosaics of events in his life. Mark's symbol is a winged lion, and as one of the four evangelists he is usually depicted holding a book and a pen.

Marzipan is said to have a link with St Mark, although the origin of marzipan is far from clear, and there are a number of possible 'explanations' of how it was first made. One legend says that a Venetian baker saved the famine-ridden city of Venice from starvation in the winter of 1407 when he discovered a cache of almonds and sugar and combined them into a nourishing 'bread'. This was dubbed 'Marci Panus' (St Mark's Bread) in honour of the city's patron saint. Other authorities suggest that the origins are much older, and that the sweet came from Arabia. In Britain 'Marci Panus' may have been transformed into the 'marchpane' dessert prized by the sugar-loving Tudors.

Whichever explanation you accept, marzipan has a long and colourful history. Because it is soft and pliable it can be shaped to create a wide variety of delicacies. Marzipan can also be easily coloured, which adds to the variety of sweetmeats that are based on it. In the eighteenth century marzipan was sometimes baked, covered with gum-water and then coated with gold leaf.

Ingredients

To make 1¹/₂ lb/700g

12oz/350g ground almonds
6oz/175g sifted icing sugar
6oz/175g caster sugar
1¹/₂ tsp lemon juice
A few drops of almond
    essence
1 lightly beaten egg

Marzipan
Method

Put the ground almonds, icing sugar and caster sugar in a mixing bowl, then add the lemon juice, almond essence and enough of the beaten egg to bind the ingredients into a fairly dry paste. Turn out onto a surface lightly dusted with icing sugar. Knead until the paste is smooth. The marzipan is now ready to be used – rolled out and used to cover a cake, or coloured and shaped to be used as petit fours or cake decorations.

Marzipan biscuits

Ingredients

4oz/100g caster sugar
3oz/75g ground almonds
Finely grated rind of a small
    orange
2 egg yolks
A few drops of almond
    essence
1oz/25g flaked almonds

This recipe uses ground almonds instead of flour. The biscuits could be individually wrapped and offered to members of the congregation when St Mark's feast day falls on a Sunday.

Method

Mix the sugar, ground almonds and orange rind in a mixing bowl. Make a well in the middle and add the egg yolks and essence, and work in the dry ingredients to form a smooth dough.

Shape into a ball, then wrap in foil and chill for about 10 minutes. Roll out the dough thinly on a surface lightly dusted with icing sugar. Cut the dough into biscuits using a 2in/5cm cutter.

Space out the biscuits on greased or lined baking sheets, sprinkle each one with a few flaked almonds, and bake in a pre-heated oven 190°C/375°F/gas mark 5 for about 10 minutes or until light golden brown. Cool on a wire rack.

St Peter
29 June

Peter, who was originally called Simon, was a fisherman on the lake of Galilee and the brother of Andrew, with whom he was called by Jesus to be a 'fisher of people'. Jesus renamed him Peter, 'the Rock' on whom he would build his Church. Peter was impetuous, hot-tempered and given to making promises he could not keep. He denied three times that he had ever known Jesus, only hours after protesting that he would never do so. But after Jesus' resurrection and ascension, when the disciples received the Holy Spirit, it was Peter who stood up and addressed the Pentecost crowd, and who became the leader of the apostles, telling the story of Jesus of Nazareth and healing the sick. He embarked on a number of missions; in Jerusalem he was imprisoned for his activities, but was released by an angel the night before his trial. In Rome he 'dictated' his memories of Jesus and his life, death and resurrection to Mark, and his recollections became the basis of Mark's Gospel. It is believed that Peter was martyred in Rome in the reign of Nero (AD54-68), probably in the gardens of the imperial palace, and tradition has it that he was crucified upside down, at his request. Excavations have established that his tomb almost certainly lies beneath the basilica of St Peter. In England many monasteries were dedicated to Peter as well as a large number of churches. In Mevagissey, Cornwall, villagers celebrate the festival of St Peter in the last week in June. Sunday schools and church congregations process to the harbour to give thanks for the harvest of the sea (the rest of the week is spent celebrating). Foods traditionally eaten at this time include saffron cake and feast buns.

To celebrate St Peter's connection with the sea, I have also included a recipe for fish pie.

Saffron cake and buns

Ingredients

To make a cake and 6-8 buns

2-3 good pinches of saffron
6 tbsp hot water
1oz/25g fresh yeast
4fl oz/125ml warm milk
1lb/400g plain flour
4oz/100g butter and lard
3oz/75g sugar
8-10oz/225-280g mixed dried
    fruit and candied peel

Saffron has always been one of the world's most expensive and sought-after spices. It was used by the Greeks, Romans and Phoenicians variously to fumigate public areas of a city, as an aphrodisiac, and to flavour cakes given to the gods. Traditionally, saffron was introduced to England in the fourteenth century by the returning Crusaders, and Saffron Walden became the main area where it was grown. Eventually it had to be imported from the East to cope with demand. The plant's golden colour and pungent flavour has been used for hundreds of years to flavour food. It is available in both filaments and powder, though it is best to use the filaments.

Method

Stir the saffron into the hot water, and soak for 20 minutes. Mix the yeast in the warm milk. Put the flour in a large mixing bowl, rub in the butter and lard and add the sugar, fruit and peel. Mix into a dough with the yeast and milk and the saffron and its water. The resultant dough should not be too firm. Knead on a floured surface. Grease the sides of a clean bowl and place the dough in the bowl, cover and leave in a warm place to rise for 2-3 hours. The fruit makes the dough heavy and so it takes some time to rise.

Divide the dough into two. Knead one piece slightly and put it in a greased loaf tin. Divide the second piece of dough into 6-8 pieces of equal size and roll into buns, then put them on a greased baking sheet. Put the loaf tin and baking sheet in plastic bags, with room for the dough to rise, and leave in a warm place for about 1 hour to prove. Bake in a pre-heated oven 190°C/375°F/gas mark 5. The buns will take about 20 minutes and the cake about 1 hour. Cool on a wire rack.

Revel buns

Ingredients

To make 20-24 buns

8oz/225g butter
1¹/₂lb/700g plain flour
1lb/450g sugar
A pinch of salt
¹/₂ tsp saffron
12oz/350g clotted cream
1 egg
1tsp ground cinnamon
1oz/25g fresh yeast
¹/₄ pint/150ml milk
6oz/175g currants

These buns were – and still are – made for celebrations of church festivals and anniversaries and it was the custom to put them on sycamore leaves before they were baked. They may have been the feast buns distributed at Mevagissey.

This recipe is the traditional, lengthy version – so start early!

Method

Rub the butter into the flour and stir in the sugar and salt, saving a teaspoonful or so to be mixed with the yeast. Tie the saffron in some muslin and let it infuse in a little warmed milk.

Warm the cream in a very low oven. Mix the yeast and reserved sugar in a little warm water. Blend the cream, flour, beaten egg and cinnamon together. Remove the saffron from the muslin and add this to the mixture together with the yeast, milk and currants. Cover and leave the mixture to rise in a warm place for 12 hours. Form the mixture into small buns and place them on a greased baking tray, then bake them in a pre-heated oven 190°C/375°F/gas mark 5 for about 30 minutes. Sprinkle a little icing sugar over the buns when they have been cooled on a wire rack.

Fish pie

Ingredients

To serve 4 people

2lb/900g cod, haddock, or any
white fish fillets. Use some
smoked fish for an extra
tasty pie
1 pint/500ml milk
3 hard-boiled eggs, shelled
and sliced
2oz/50g butter
2oz/50g flour
2 tbsp chopped fresh parsley
1 tsp chopped capers
Salt and pepper
1lb/400g mashed potatoes

As Peter was a fisherman what better way to celebrate than with a tasty fish pie?
The fish used in this dish can vary according to availability and price.

Method

Cook the fish in the milk in a saucepan. Drain the fish and reserve the milk. Remove the skin and flake the fish into a 2-2$\frac{1}{2}$ pint/1-1.25 litre pie dish, then lay the slices of egg on top of the fish. Melt the butter in a saucepan and stir in the flour, then add the reserved milk and cook until the sauce thickens. Stir in the parsley, capers and season. Pour the sauce over the eggs and fish, and cover with the mashed potato. Use a fork to create 'waves' on the surface of the pie. Cook in a pre-heated oven 190°C/375°F/gas mark 5 for about 30 minutes, until the potato is light brown. Sliced tomatoes can be layered on top of the eggs.

St James
25 July

James was the son of Zebedee and the brother of John, and both were fishermen who were mending their nets when Jesus called them to follow him. James was one of the three apostles who witnessed the transfiguration of Christ and the agony in the Garden of Gethsemane. According to Spanish tradition James travelled to Spain and preached the gospel there, though there is no concrete evidence of this. His reputed burial place and particular site of pilgrimage is Santiago de Compostela; many pilgrims travelled there to honour his memory, and many miracles were attributed to him. In art James is often represented with his emblems of a pilgrim's hat and a scallop shell, so to celebrate his feast day, I have included a recipe for scallops in this section.

St James' Day is celebrated in St Ives, Cornwall, with a special ceremony held every five years. This commemorates a former mayor of the town, John Knill, who erected a mausoleum for himself on a hill above the town, though when the time came he was never actually buried there. He left money for the upkeep of the mausoleum, and money to be distributed to pilchard fishermen who had done particularly well in their work.

The ceremony is still celebrated with a procession to the Guildhall and the singing of the Old Hundredth psalm. Stargazy pie was a local Cornish dish, and so, as James too was a fisherman, I have added a recipe for it to this section.

Baked scallops

Ingredients

To serve 4 people

8 scallops, prepared as
    described (keep the shells
    for serving)
$1/4$ pint/125ml fish stock
1 small onion, peeled and
    quartered
Salt and pepper
1 bay leaf
$1/4$ pint/125ml cheese sauce
2oz/50g grated Cheddar
    cheese

Scallops are sold fresh in their opened shells or can
be bought shelled and frozen. To prepare the
scallop, scrape off the surrounding fringe, or beard,
and the black intestinal thread. The white part of
the scallop is the flesh, the orange part is the coral
or roe, and both parts are edible. Next, ease the
flesh and coral from the flat shell with a short,
strong knife. Wash the scallop and drain dry.

Method

Put the prepared scallops in an ovenproof dish with the
stock, onion, seasoning and bay leaf. Cover the dish with
a lid or greased paper and bake in a pre-heated oven
180°C/350°F/gas mark 4 for about 10 minutes.
Carefully remove the scallops from the dish with a slotted
spoon and replace them in their shells. Heat the cheese
sauce with the cooking liquor and spoon a little sauce
over the scallops, sprinkle a little of the grated cheese on
the top of each scallop and brown under the grill until
the sauce bubbles.
Serve the scallops with creamed potatoes and salad.

Stargazy pie

Ingredients

To serve 6-8 people

8 pilchards or 12 large
  sardines, cleaned and
  boned and seasoned with
  salt and pepper inside
1 large onion, peeled and
  chopped
2 heaped tbsp of chopped
  fresh herbs
8 rashers streaky bacon, rinds
  removed
6 tbsp milk
1/2 tsp saffron filaments
  (optional)
12oz/350g shortcrust pastry

This pie is so named because the heads of the pilchards protrude through the pastry to gaze heavenwards. The heads are not eaten, but because they are left on the fish the useful fish oil drains down the pilchard into the part of the fish to be eaten.

Method

Mix the onions and the herbs together and put a little of this mixture inside each fish, pressing the sides of the fish together.

Cut the bacon so that there is enough to put between the fish when you make the pie. If you are using saffron put it in the milk, bring to the boil then leave to infuse and cool. Roll out half the pastry quite thinly to line a large greased ovenproof plate. Scatter any unused onion and herb mixture over the pastry. Brush the rim of the pastry with saffron or plain milk. Lay the fish on the pastry, cut side down, so that the heads lie on the rim of the pastry, put the bacon in the gaps between the fish, and season with salt and pepper.

Roll out the rest of the pastry, slightly thicker than the bottom half, and cut a circle the size of the plate. Lay this over the pie, tuck it back to expose the fish heads and press down to seal the pie between them.

Bake in a pre-heated oven 200°C/400°F/gas mark 6 for 15 minutes, then lower the heat to 180°C/360°F/gas mark 4 and cook for a further 30 minutes.

Braised Ebernoe lamb

Ingredients

4lb/2kg shoulder of lamb
1oz/25g dripping
3 rashers streaky bacon,
    chopped, with the rind
    removed
8oz/225g onions, peeled and
    sliced
8oz/225g carrots, peeled and
    sliced
4oz/100g turnip or swede,
    peeled and diced
2 sticks celery, washed,
    trimmed and diced
$1/2$ pint/300ml stock
A little parsley, basil, thyme
    and rosemary freshly
    chopped
Salt

Ebernoe, a small village in West Sussex, used to hold a fair on St James' Day. Among the various traditional festivities was a cricket match and the roasting of a whole ram. The batsman who scored the most runs in the match was presented with a horn from the ram's head. The name of the fair thus changed from St James' Fair to Ebernoe Horn Fair, which is commemorated in this dish.

Method

Use a large hob-to-oven casserole with a well-fitting lid when you make this dish. Remove the fat from the shoulder of lamb. Heat the dripping in the casserole and start to fry the bacon. Before it goes brown add the vegetables and continue to fry until the fat is absorbed. Stir frequently whilst the vegetables are cooking.

Pour in the stock, herbs and seasoning, bring to the boil, then place the lamb on top of the vegetables. Then reduce the heat, put the lid on the casserole and simmer for 2 hours. Remove from the heat, take off the lid and continue to cook the casserole in the middle of a pre-heated oven 220°C/425°F/gas mark 7 for 30 minutes or until the top of the lamb is brown and crispy.

Transfer the meat and vegetables to a warmed serving dish and keep warm. Pour the remaining stock into a saucepan and simmer until the volume is reduced by half. Pour the stock over the meat and serve with more vegetables if required.

St Oswald
9 August

Oswald was born in 605, and for the early part of his life he was in exile from his father Ethelfrith's kingdom of Northumbria on the island of Iona, where he became a Christian. In 633 returned, to defeat the Welsh King Cadwallon of Gwynedd in a battle near Hexham, so restoring his father's kingdom. Oswald then sent for missionaries from Iona to carry out the evangelization of Northumbria. The missionaries were led by St Aidan, whose friendship with Oswald resulted in an effective partnership, as Oswald became Aidan's interpreter. Oswald married Cyneburga, daughter of Cynegils, the first Christian king of Wessex, and this gave him some power over the other English kingdoms. Sadly, eight years later, Oswald was killed by the pagan King Penda of Mercia at the battle of Maselferth (possibly Oswestry). Tradition says that as he was dying Oswald was heard to pray for the souls of the men who fell with him.

An ancient ceremony to mark St Oswald's Day still takes place in Grasmere in the Lake District, and a few other northern villages, on the Saturday nearest to 9 August. A procession of people carrying rushes wends its way to the church to scatter the rushes on the floor, which in centuries past was a way of keeping the church floor clean and warm. The Grasmere church floor was paved with flagstones in the nineteenth century so the rushes are no longer needed, but the ceremony survives. The rush-bearers are each given a piece of gingerbread stamped with the name of St Oswald, and the children are given a coin to spend at the local gingerbread shop.

The recipe for this gingerbread is a closely guarded secret known only to the bakers at the Grasmere Gingerbread Shop, so the recipe here is for Grasmere gingerbread cake instead. You will find a recipe for gingerbread in the St Giles section (see p. 132).

Ingredients

4oz/100g butter
4oz/100g sugar
3 eggs
10oz/280g plain flour
1 tsp baking powder
$1/4$ tsp ground ginger
3oz/75g preserved ginger
1 tbsp syrup from the
    preserved ginger
A little grated lemon rind

Grasmere gingerbread cake
Method

Cream the butter and sugar together, then add the eggs separately, beating the mixture between each addition. Stir in the flour, baking powder and ground ginger. Cut the preserved ginger into small pieces and stir into the mixture together with the ginger syrup and lemon rind. Grease or line a suitable tin and pour in the mixture and bake in a pre-heated oven for $1^3/_4$ hours at 120°-170C/250-325°F/gas mark 1-3. Cool on a wire rack and cut into squares.

Ingredients

8oz/200g flour
4oz/100g soft brown sugar
$1/2$ tsp ground ginger
$1/4$ tsp baking powder
4oz/100g butter

Filling

4oz/100g icing sugar
2oz/50g butter
$1/2$ tsp ground ginger
A little preserved ginger
    (finely chopped)
1 tsp syrup from the preserved
    ginger

Grasmere shortcake

A variation on the above.

Method

Place the dry ingredients in a mixing bowl and rub in the butter. Grease or line a shallow baking tin, tip the mixture into the tin and spread it evenly, pressing down lightly. Bake in a pre-heated oven at 200°C/400°F/gas mark 6, until golden brown. Turn out and trim the edges. Cut into two equally sized pieces whilst still hot. These can be kept, when cool, in an airtight tin, and the filling added later.

To make the filling, beat the butter and icing sugar into a creamy mixture and add the chopped ginger and syrup. Spread the filling evenly on one of the shortbread pieces and gently press the other piece on top. Cut into pieces with a sharp knife.

St Bartholomew
24 August

Bartholomew is named in the Gospels of Matthew, Mark and Luke as one of the apostles, though in John's Gospel he is referred to as Nathanael. He was probably one and the same person. He came from Galilee, and Jesus described him as 'truly an Israelite in whom there is no deceit'. Bartholomew may have been a missionary to 'India' which at that time could also have meant Arabia or Ethiopia, and he may also have visited and taught the people of Asia Minor. Roman martyrology records that he was flayed alive and beheaded; his relics are said to be in the church of St Bartholomew in Rome.

Many churches in England were dedicated to him, and Bart's Hospital in London is named after him.

Bartholomew is the patron saint of bee-keepers and traditionally honey is harvested on his feast day. In Cornwall mead-makers still bring mead to be blessed in the church at Mounts Bay, near Penzance. Bartholomew Fair, at Smithfield in London, was held on 24 August from 1133 until 1855. Apples coated in honey were sold here, an early version of our toffee apples.

At Sandwich in Kent, a memorial service for the hospital founders is held at St Bartholomew's Hospital (almshouses). One of the hospital's 16 residents is elected 'Master' for the day. After the church service children race around the chapel for the reward of a currant bun, and all the adults present are given a souvenir of a St Bartholomew's biscuit, bearing the stamp of the hospital's seal.

Honey cake

Ingredients

To make a cake 9in/23cm diameter or 8in/20cm square.

3oz/75g butter
3oz/75g sugar
2 eggs, beaten
4oz/100g honey
8oz/225g self-raising flour, sifted
1 tsp baking powder

This cake is widely enjoyed in Britain; the Scots use their local heather honey and the Welsh their local honey and cinnamon. Clover and heather honey give the cake a distinctive flavour; in fact any flavoured honey will add something special to your cake. Dried fruit and nuts are sometimes also added. If the honey used has a high water content the cake may sink a little and whilst this may not look up to your usual standard the cake will taste delicious.

Method

Cream together the butter and sugar, then gradually add the beaten eggs and honey, and work in the flour and baking powder. Mix well. Put the mixture in a greased and/or lined cake tin. Bake in a pre-heated oven 180°C/350°F/gas mark 4 for 45-50 minutes. Cool on a wire rack.

Ingredients

7oz/175g icing sugar
2 eggs
6oz/150g honey, warmed
15oz/425g flour
1tsp each of bicarbonate of soda, ground ginger, cinnamon, nutmeg and cloves

Honey cake biscuits

These biscuits are soft, spicy biscuits that keep well in an airtight tin.

Method

Sift together the flour and bicarbonate of soda in a separate bowl. Whisk the eggs and sugar together until the mixture is thick and creamy, then add the spices and warm honey to the egg mixture, beating all the time. Beat in the flour. Turn the mixture out onto a lightly floured surface and knead until smooth.
Chill for at least 3 hours, preferably covered, in the refrigerator. Knead again, roll out to about 1/4in/5mm thick and cut into shapes as desired. Pierce the biscuits in the centre with a knitting needle and brush the surface with egg. Bake in a pre-heated oven 200°C/400°F/ gas mark 6 for 7 minutes.

Mead

Ingredients

To make 8 pints/4.5 litres

2oz/50g root ginger
8 pints/4.5 litres water
3lb/1.5kg light honey
Juice and thinly peeled rind of
   2 lemons
1oz/25g mead or baker's yeast

Mead, made from fermented honey, is one of the world's oldest drinks, and it has been drunk for many centuries in Britain. Flavoured honey and sweet herbs, such as cloves, ginger or cinnamon, give the mead a delicate bouquet, but these must be added sparingly so that the honey flavour is not overpowered. Soft water is best for mead making. The honey water should not be boiled for any length of time.

Method

Put the ginger root in a clean cloth and bruise it, using a wooden spoon, to release the flavour. Tie the ginger and lemon rind in a piece of muslin and put it in a 12 pint/ 6.8 litre saucepan. Pour on the water and lemon juice and heat to boiling point.

Leave to cool to 50°C/122°F. Whilst this cools stand the honey in a warm place so that it reaches the same temperature. Add the honey to the water and ginger and mix together. Leave to cool to 21°C/70°F. Now remove the ginger and crumble the yeast into the syrup. Pour this mixture into a demi-john, fit an airlock and leave until fermentation has stopped. Leave for a further couple of weeks before bottling. Mead can be used after 4-6 months, but it improves on keeping for several years.

Toffee apples

Ingredients

To make 8 toffee apples

8 small eating apples
8 wooden skewers

For the toffee

8oz/225g soft brown sugar
1oz/25g unsalted butter
1 tbsp golden syrup
5 tbsp water
1 tsp vinegar

From the middle of the seventeenth century sugar has been imported in bulk, but it was initially very expensive. Any craving for sweetness the poorer people might have had to be satisfied by honey or treacle. Nevertheless toffee apples were sold at fairs and markets. The apples used were usually little windfalls and they were dipped in a sticky mixture of honey with some beeswax.

Method

Thoroughly wash and dry the apples, remove the stalks and push a skewer into the centre of each apple.

Put the toffee ingredients in a heavy-based saucepan and heat the mixture gently until the sugar is dissolved. Bring the toffee to the boil and cook until it reaches 143°C /290°F or until a drop of toffee put into a bowl of cold water snaps cleanly.

Dip the apples in the toffee, twisting them so they are completely coated, dip them at once into a bowl of cold/iced water and then put them onto a greased tray.

When the toffee is set hard wrap the toffee apples in cellophane or plastic film.

Ingredients

To make 6 buns

8oz/225g strong white flour
$1/_2$ tsp salt
$1/_2$oz/15g margarine
$1/_2$oz/15g fresh yeast
$1/_2$ tsp sugar
1 50mg vitamin C tablet
4fl oz/115ml milk, warmed
1 egg, beaten
3oz/75g mixed dried fruit
1oz/25g candied peel
2oz/50g light brown sugar
1oz/25g butter, melted
A square greased 9in/23cm tin

For the glaze

1 tbsp caster sugar
2 tbsp milk

Chelsea buns
Method

This is the quick method for the recipe. Sift the flour and salt into a mixing bowl, and rub in the margarine. Mix the yeast and sugar and crushed vitamin C tablet in the warmed milk in a small jug or basin and pour into the centre of the flour, together with the beaten egg. Mix to form a dough and knead for 2-3 minutes in a food mixer, or for 5 or more minutes by hand.

Roll/shape the dough on a floured surface to form a rectangle about 9x9in/23x23cms. Brush the surface of the dough with the melted butter, and sprinkle over the brown sugar and the dried fruit and peel. Now roll up the dough to form a Swiss roll.

Cut the roll into slices about $1^1/_2$in/4cm thick, and arrange them on a square greased 9in/23cm tin, cut side up, allowing space for the buns to expand. Cover and put in a warm place to prove for about 30 minutes. Bake in a pre-heated oven 220°C/425°F/gas mark 7 for 20 minutes or until golden brown. While the buns are still hot glaze them with sugar dissolved in the milk. A little extra caster sugar may be sprinkled over the buns if liked.

Dear Lord, thank you for this food.
Bless the hands that prepared it.
Bless it to our use and us to your service.
And make us ever mindful of the needs of others.
Through Christ our Lord we pray.

Traditional

Lord Jesus, be our holy guest,
Our morning joy, our evening rest,
And with our daily bread impart
Your love and peace to every heart.

Anonymous

St Giles
1 September

Although Giles was one of the most popular saints in Western Europe in the later Middle Ages, very little is known about him. He is thought to have lived as a hermit in a remote area of Provence, near the mouth of the River Rhone, and died around 710. He is known to have been a healer, and legend has it that he healed a beggar by wrapping him in his own cloak. Through his care for others he is the patron saint of the lame and of lepers. As lepers were banned from entering medieval towns for fear of infection, small leper settlements often developed just outside the walls. Many churches built there by the people who cared for them were dedicated to St Giles. In England alone over 160 early churches were dedicated to him as well as 24 hospitals. The best known churches in Britain named after him are St Giles' Cathedral in Edinburgh and St Giles', Cripplegate in London.

St Giles' feast day is celebrated on 1 September and several towns, such as Oxford and Barnstaple (Devon) have St Giles' Fairs at this time. Today's fairs have changed a great deal from the original celebrations. Oxford's fair is held on the Monday and Tuesday after the first Sunday after St Giles' feast day. Today it bears little resemblance to the original fair, and is largely a pleasure fair. The fair at Barnstaple has undergone changes over the centuries too, and now always begins on the Wednesday preceding the 20 September (so it has moved from St Giles' Day). Originally the fair would have come at the end of a big annual market and lasted a week; now it lasts for four days. The ceremony at the start of the fair, however, survives from ancient times. The Town Council meets in the Guildhall where various toasts are drunk in spiced ale and fairings are eaten. Gingerbread and Barnstaple fair pears were once included in the festivities. At 12 noon the civic procession forms up at High Cross near the Guildhall, and a proclamation is read out. This is repeated at two more points in the town.

At such celebrations and fairs the biscuits that were usually sold or given away were naturally called 'fairings'. These biscuits were only one of the many sweet treats sold at fairs and local recipes varied around the country; they included ginger fairings sweetened with honey, which gives a distinctive flavour. Crisp ginger biscuits were a later adaptation.

Ingredients

8oz/200g flour
2 tsp baking powder
2 tsp bicarbonate of soda
2 tsp mixed spice
3 tsp ground ginger
1 tsp cinnamon
$\frac{1}{2}$ tsp salt
4oz/100g butter
4oz/100g sugar
4 tbsp golden syrup

Fairings
Method

Sift the dry ingredients into a bowl, rub in the butter, stir in the sugar, then pour in the warmed golden syrup and mix thoroughly. Roll the mixture into small balls and place them well spaced on greased baking sheets.
Bake in a pre-heated oven 200°C/400°F/gas mark 6, and as they start to brown move them to a lower shelf to finish cooking and become golden brown. Remove from the baking sheets and cool on a wire rack.

Ingredients

4oz/100g butter
4oz/100g sugar
4 tbsp golden syrup
8oz/200g flour
2 tsp baking powder
2 tsp bicarbonate of soda
2 tsp mixed spice
3 tsp ground ginger
1 tsp cinnamon
$\frac{1}{2}$ tsp salt

Ginger fairings
Method

Melt the butter, sugar and syrup. Sift the dry ingredients into a bowl and stir in the melted mixture to form a dough. Roll the dough into small balls and place them on greased baking sheets. Bake in a pre-heated oven 200°C/400°F/gas mark 6 for 10-15 minutes or until golden brown. Remove them from the baking sheets and cool on a wire rack.

Barnstaple fair pears

Ingredients

To serve 4 people

4 large, firm Comice pears
1oz/25g blanched almonds,
  split in half
2oz/50g caster sugar
$^1/_2$ pint/300ml red wine
2 cloves

The owners of local pear orchards used to supply the stallholders at the annual St Giles Fair with these pears, which would originally have been simmered in local cider or scrumpy. Served with clotted cream they make a delicious dessert.

Method

Peel the pears, leaving the stalks on. Spike the pears with the almond pieces. Put the sugar, wine and cloves in a saucepan that will be large enough to hold the pears. Gently heat the wine until the sugar is dissolved.
Add the pears, standing them upright, then cover the saucepan and simmer for 15 minutes, or until the pears are just tender. Baste the pears with the wine from time to time throughout the 15 minutes.
Remove the pears from the pan with a slotted spoon and place them on a serving dish. Boil the syrup in the uncovered pan until the volume is reduced by half. Pour the syrup over the pears and serve either hot or cold with clotted cream or thick natural yoghurt.

Ingredients

8oz/225g plain flour
4 level tsp ground
   ginger
4oz/100g margarine
4oz/100g brown sugar
4oz/100g black treacle
4oz/100g golden syrup
1/2 pint/140ml milk
1 tsp bicarbonate of
   soda
1 egg

Gingerbread

This recipe makes a lovely sticky, moist gingerbread.

Method

Sift the flour and ginger into a mixing bowl.
Melt together margarine, sugar, treacle, syrup and milk until the sugar dissolves, then quickly stir in the bicarbonate of soda.
Add the egg to the dry ingredients and when this is mixed in pour in the warmed ingredients and mix very thoroughly.
Pour the mixture into a greased and lined 7in/18cm square tin, but use a larger one if thinner slices are preferred. Bake in a pre-heated oven 150°C/300°F/gas mark 2 for 1-1 1/2 hours. Cool on a wire rack.
Although this can be eaten immediately the stickiness increases when stored for a few days in an airtight tin.

Brandy snaps

Ingredients

2oz/50g butter
2oz/50g demerara sugar
2oz/50g golden syrup
1/2 tsp ground ginger
2oz/50g plain flour, sifted
1/2 tsp lemon juice

In medieval times these crispy curls were called 'gauffres' or wafers. They were sold at many of the fairs together with the fairings and gingerbread.

Method

Line two baking sheets with baking paper. Gently warm the butter, sugar, syrup and ginger in a thick-based saucepan, until the butter is melted and the sugar dissolved. Remove from the heat and stir in the flour and lemon juice. Put generous teaspoonfuls on the baking sheets, very well spaced out as the mixture will spread.
Bake for 15 minutes in a pre-heated oven 220°C/425°F/gas mark 7. Before the discs cool, lift each one with a palette knife and whilst still warm roll it around the greased handle of a wooden spoon. Allow the curls to cool on a wire tray. The brandy snaps can be eaten on their own or filled with ginger flavoured whipped cream.

St Michael
29 September

Michael the Archangel has been venerated throughout Christian history. He has been honoured as 'the captain of the heavenly host' (see Revelation 12.7-9), and the protector of Christians, particularly soldiers. In the East he is regarded as a special helper of the sick. Visions of Michael have long been associated with hilltops – from Monte Gargono in southern Italy between 492 and 496, to the legends associated with Mont-Saint Michel in France, and to a similar but vague story connected to St Michael's Mount in Cornwall.

The third Quarter Day of the farming year also falls on Michaelmas, 29 September. It was the custom for tenants to present their landlords, together with their rent, a goose fattened on the grain in the stubble fields. The Michaelmas goose was then enjoyed by everyone to celebrate the feast day.

Although turkey has replaced goose for many people at the Christmas festive meal, some people still prefer goose. In earlier years it would have been stuffed with all the fruits and herbs available, or possibly just with potatoes. It would also be served with a spicy wine sauce, if finances allowed.

At Michaelmas bannocks were also a speciality (see recipes in the St Brigid section, p. 100).

Stuffed goose

Although this is an old recipe it would have been a luxury because prunes, at one time an expensive item, are used for the stuffing. In this recipe the prunes have replaced the quinces, pears, grapes and garlic that would have been cheaper and more readily available.

Ingredients

To serve 8 people

1 goose, about 10lbs/4.5kg
Salt and pepper
1lb/450g prunes, soaked overnight
    (if necessary), stoned and chopped
1lb/450g apples, peeled, cored and
    chopped
2oz/50g soft brown sugar
$\frac{1}{2}$ pint/300ml chicken stock
1 pint/600ml dry cider
2 tbsp redcurrant jelly

Bread sauce

Ingredients

$\frac{1}{2}$ pint/275ml milk
1 onion, peeled
6 cloves
2-3oz/50-75g fresh white
    breadcrumbs
Salt and pepper

Method

Pour the milk into a saucepan, stab the onion with the cloves and put the onion in the milk. Simmer until the onion is soft. Remove the onion from the milk and add the breadcrumbs to obtain the consistency you want. Season with salt and pepper. The onion can be finely chopped (cloves removed) and added to the sauce if you prefer.

Method

Wash and wipe the goose, having first removed the giblets. Prick the skin all over and season inside and out with salt and pepper.

Mix the prunes, apples and sugar together and put into the body cavity of the goose. Secure with a skewer. Place the bird on a rack in a roasting tin and cook in the centre of a pre-heated oven 190°C/375°F/gas mark 5 for about $3\frac{1}{2}$ hrs (20 minutes per lb/450g plus 50 minutes). Mix the stock and cider together in a saucepan and bring to the boil. After the bird has been in the oven for about 30 minutes reduce the heat to 170°C/325°F/gas mark 3. Now start to baste the goose every 20 minutes with the stock and cider mixture until it is all used up. To test if the goose is cooked pierce the leg flesh with a sharp knife and if the juice that comes out is clear the goose is cooked and can be put on a warm serving dish.

Drain the fat off the liquid in the cooking pan and dissolve the redcurrant jelly in the remaining juices. Bring this gravy to the boil and add more cider if more gravy will be needed. Serve the goose with the gravy, apple or gooseberry sauce and bread sauce.

Alternative stuffings include rum-soaked apple with sage, potato, or bacon and sausage meat.

Goose can be served cold with a selection of fresh vegetables, leftover stuffing and pickles.

134

Spiced bramble jelly

Ingredients

To make 2-3lbs/900g-1.4kg of jelly

4lb/1.8kg blackberries
2¹/₂fl oz/75ml water
Juice of 2 lemons
Sugar
Ground mixed spice

This recipe is included here because of an old saying that blackberries should not be picked after 28 September. On the first St Michael's Day Satan is said to have fallen into a bramble bush when he was cast out of heaven, so now Satan wanders the countryside on the anniversary, blasting the blackberries with his breath or spitting on them. So, pick them before and celebrate St Michael's Day with the ever-popular blackberry and apple pie or, if there is a glut, make some of this spiced bramble jelly to enjoy during the coming months. The fruit can also be frozen and used to make pies or other desserts when the weather gets cold: a reminder of sunny autumn days.

Method

Wash the blackberries and put into a large, heavy-based saucepan with the water and lemon juice. Bring to the boil and simmer for 15-20 minutes, or until the berries are tender. Strain through a jelly bag for 2-3 hours.

Measure the strained juice and weigh out 1lb/450g of sugar and 1 teaspoon of spice for every pint (575-600ml) of juice. Put the sugar into an ovenproof dish and warm through in a cool oven 110°C/225°F/gas mark 1, which will take about 10-15 minutes. Pour the juice back in the saucepan and heat gently, then add the warmed sugar and spice, stirring until the sugar has dissolved. Bring to the boil and cook rapidly for 12-15 minutes or until the setting point is reached.

To test the setting point put about 1 teaspoonful of the jelly on a saucer and put it to cool in the refrigerator for about 1 minute. Then gently pull a finger over the surface of the jelly and if it wrinkles the setting point has been reached. Pour the jelly into warmed jars and seal.

Farmhouse fry

Ingredients

4 rashers streaky bacon, rinds
  removed
2oz/50g butter
4 medium onions, peeled and
  sliced
2 pig's kidneys or lamb's
  kidneys, skinned and cored
8oz/225g pig's or lamb's liver,
  cut into 4 thin slices
4 small pork chops or lamb
  cutlets
1oz/25g seasoned flour
4 tomatoes, skinned and
  halved
8oz/225g mushrooms, sliced
2 large slices white bread,
  crusts removed

Long before mixed grills appeared the wealthier yeomen used to celebrate the Michaelmas killing of surplus stock with a fry-up of the offal from the animals. Offal could not be preserved and kept for later on, so kidneys, liver and brains were put into a large frying pan with a chop or two and some bacon. In the north of England black and white puddings were added.

Method

For this recipe you will need 2 large frying pans and a warm serving dish.

Heat both frying pans and put the bacon in one and the butter in the other. Fry the onions slowly in the butter. Once the bacon starts to crisp take the rashers out and keep them hot on the serving dish.

If pig's kidneys are to be used cut them in half. Dip the kidneys, liver slices and chops or cutlets in the seasoned flour, then fry them in the bacon pan, cooking the meat thoroughly. If you cannot cook the meat in one go, fry the chops first, then the liver and the kidneys last.

As the onions cook, turn them from time to time. When thy are done, push them to one side of the pan then add and fry the tomatoes and mushrooms.

When all the meat and vegetables are cooked arrange them on the serving dish and keep hot.

Pour any fat and juice from the vegetable pan into the bacon pan. Cut the slices of bread in half and quickly fry until the bread is crisp and golden brown on both sides. Arrange on the dish and serve immediately.

St Teresa of Avila
15 October

Teresa was born in Avila in 1515, as Teresa de Cepeda y Ahumada, into a well-to-do noble family. When she was about 20 she became a nun of the Carmelite order and she entered the Convent of the Incarnation in Avila. To begin with Teresa found convent life difficult – she missed her family and suffered with ill-health. But she persevered and gradually began to make headway in her spiritual life, experiencing mystical visions. In middle age, with encouragement from others, she founded her own convent of St Joseph, based on the original strict Carmelite Rule. It was the first house of 'discalced' (barefooted) Carmelites; followers of the more relaxed Rule were known as 'calced' (shod). Teresa travelled widely throughout Spain during the following years, visiting other religious houses, and despite much opposition she succeeded in having the Discalced Carmelites separated into an Order of their own. She founded 17 other convents and also worked with St John of the Cross to found convents of friars. Teresa combined a deep spirituality with practical wisdom and common sense, and she understood very well the difficulties of life in community. 'If the nuns are melancholy,' she is reputed to have said, 'let them eat steak!' Her influence spread far beyond Spain, and her writings have helped countless people to discover the spiritual life for themselves. In 1970 Pope Paul VI named her as a Doctor of the Church, the first woman to be so honoured.

Fillet of beef with tomatoes

Ingredients

1¼lb/550g fillet steak cut into
 ¾in/1.5cm thick fillets
2oz/50g butter
8oz/250g tomatoes
1oz/25g flour
½ pint/300ml stock
Salt and pepper

As tomatoes were available in the sixteenth century people of that time would have been able to cook this recipe if they had sufficient resources.

Method

Coat the steaks in seasoned flour and fry in the butter until brown, turning the meat to cook both sides.

Cut the tomatoes into thick slices, put them in a tin and cook them in a slow oven for a few minutes.

Fry any tomato trimmings in the butter and juices remaining in the frying pan, stir in the flour and add the stock, season and boil the gravy to cook the flour. Strain the gravy.

Arrange the fillets along the centre of a hot serving dish and place a slice of tomato between each. Garnish with the remaining tomato slices and surround the steaks with the strained gravy.

St Martin of Tours
11 November

Martin was born around 315 in what is now Hungary. He was a soldier's son and followed his father into the Roman army, becoming a member of the Imperial Guard. The most well-known story about him is that when a young officer he cut his cloak in half and gave it to a starving beggar. Soon afterwards he was baptized and applied for his discharge from the army, saying that he could not be a disciple of Christ and fight others. After some time spent as a recluse he became a disciple of Hilary of Poitiers, founding a religious community at Ligugé, the first in Gaul. Martin was made Bishop of Tours in about 370, living at first in a solitary place nearby, which attracted followers to him. Eventually this became the monastery of Marmoutier.

Martin was a very active missionary, travelling widely on foot, by donkey and by boat. He was outspoken in his condemnation of paganism, smashing idols and pagan sites if he thought it necessary. Many churches were named after him: St Martin's Church in Canterbury was consecrated by St Augustine, and St-Martin-in-the Fields in London continues his work among the poor and homeless.

St Martin's Summer (if it occurs!) is a spell of fine weather around the time of Martin's feast day in November. It was once a time for slaughtering cattle, which could not all be kept through the lean winter months. Some beef was dried and smoked, and was called 'Martinmas Beef'. Meat was also pickled or salted so that it could still be eaten through the winter months.

In Scotland Martinmas was the first day of the farm workers' holiday and a day of celebration, when the farmer gave his workers meat from a recently slaughtered ox, often as haggis, black pudding or white pudding. The farm workers and their families would have made the most of this by making a pot roast or a stew to serve as many people as possible. Today haggis and black and white pudding can all be bought quite readily in good butchers' shops and supermarkets.

Martinmas was also the time for many hiring fairs and there was much movement of labour. In Scotland the farm labourers who were moving on, especially the ploughmen, would entertain those who were staying to a Martinmas Foy, which was a simple meal of bread, cheese and whisky.

Ingredients

To serve 4-6 people

2½lb-3lb/1.1-1.4 kg topside or
    fresh silverside of beef
2oz/50g butter, melted
2 large onions, peeled and
    quartered
8oz/225g carrots, peeled and
    sliced
1 medium turnip or swede,
    peeled and sliced
1 tsp fresh thyme
1 clove garlic, crushed
½ pint/275-300ml stock
¼ pint/150ml red wine
Salt and pepper
Additional vegetables such as
    broad beans, peas,
    mushrooms (optional)

Pot roast beef
Method

Fry the beef on all sides in the butter to brown well. Set it aside and fry the onions, carrots and turnip or swede in the remaining butter until they begin to brown. Put the vegetables in a large, deep casserole and place the meat on top of them. Sprinkle the beef with the thyme and garlic, season and pour on the stock and wine. Cover the casserole with a lid or foil. Cook in a pre-heated oven 180°C/350°F/gas mark 4, for at least 1½ hours or until the meat is tender. Remove the lid or foil and add the additional vegetables for the last 20 minutes, which will also allow the meat to brown.

Arrange the meat on a flat serving dish with the vegetables around it, and the gravy separately in a gravy boat. Mashed potatoes go well with this dish.

Ingredients

2lb/900g shin of beef, cut into 1in/2.5cm cubes
$1\frac{1}{2}$oz/40g flour seasoned with salt and pepper
2oz/50g beef dripping
8oz/225g onions, peeled and sliced
1 pint/575-600ml stock
$\frac{1}{2}$ pint/275-300ml cider
Salt and pepper
8oz/225g carrots, peeled and diced
8oz/225g turnips, peeled and diced
2 sticks celery, cleaned and diced
12 parsley dumplings

Beef casserole

Dumplings date back at least to the sixteenth century. In Essex it was traditional to serve plain suet pudding and gravy before the meat course, perhaps to take the edge off people's appetites so they would not want so much meat! Other variations include the addition of currants or herbs. In Devon parsley is sometimes put into the dumplings, which are especially tasty with a cider-based stew. Other perhaps less appetising variations used bread dough or pancake batter.

Method

Coat the meat cubes in the seasoned flour. Heat the dripping in a large, heavy-based saucepan, cook the onions until they are transparent then add the meat and cook until it is brown. Add the stock and cider, incorporating all the flour mixture that may be left in the pan. Season with salt and pepper.
Bring the stew to the boil and then remove any fat that may form on the surface. Add the carrots, turnips and celery and bring to the boil again, then simmer for $2\frac{1}{2}$ hours. The stew could be transferred to a slow cooker and cooked until the meat is tender. Make the dumplings and place them on top of the stew to cook for the last 20 minutes.

Parsley dumplings
Ingredients

To make 8-12 dumplings

4oz/100g self-raising flour
4oz/100g fresh white breadcrumbs
2 tbsp shredded suet – beef or vegetable
1 tbsp finely chopped parsley
2 tsp finely grated lemon rind
Salt and pepper
1 egg, beaten

Method

Put the flour, breadcrumbs, suet, parsley and lemon rind in a mixing bowl and mix them together with a wooden spoon. Season with salt and pepper and bind together with the egg to form a soft dough. Use floured hands to mould the dough into small balls the size of large walnuts. Cook them on top of the stew.

Fair cakes

Ingredients
For the pastry

1lb/400g flour
8oz/200g butter
1 dssp sugar
$\frac{1}{2}$oz/15g fresh yeast
$\frac{1}{2}$ cup warm water
A pinch of salt

For the filling

1lb/400g currants
8oz/200g soft brown sugar
2oz/50g candied peel, finely
    chopped
$\frac{1}{4}$ tsp ground nutmeg
$\frac{1}{4}$ tsp mixed spice
1 tsp rum

These were made for the hiring fairs, especially those held at Whitsun and Martinmas.

Method

Rub the butter into the flour in a mixing bowl add salt, stir in the sugar and make a well in the middle. Pour in the yeast mixed in the warm water. Mix together to form a dough. Roll out the dough very thinly and cut into 4-5in/10-12cm (110-140mm) squares. Mix the ingredients for the filling together and add a little water (or more rum) if the filling is too dry. Put a tablespoonful of the filling onto half the squares, dampen the edges with water and cover with the remaining squares of pastry, sealing the edges by pinching together. Bake in a hot oven until the cakes are golden brown.

Lamb pie

Ingredients

2 lamb cutlets
2 lambs' kidneys, skinned and
    cored
1lb/450g leeks, trimmed,
    washed and cut into
    1in/2.5cm slices
1$\frac{1}{2}$lb small potatoes, peeled
    and sliced $\frac{1}{2}$in/1.5cm thick
1oz/25g seasoned flour
$\frac{1}{2}$ tsp dried thyme
$\frac{1}{2}$ tsp dried rosemary
Salt and pepper
1 pint/575-600ml chicken stock
12oz/350g shortcrust pastry

Various recipes were used to make lamb pies, which were popular at many fairs up and down the country. Each fair may well have had its own speciality. One recipe uses minced lamb or mutton, currants and sugar. This recipe is for a more orthodox version of the St Martin's lamb pies especially popular in Wales.

Method

Trim the cutlets, leaving the bone in. If leg meat is used remove the skin, fat and bone and cut into 1in/2.5cm cubes. Coat the meat in seasoned flour and place in the bottom of a greased pie dish. Sprinkle the meat with the herbs. Cut the kidneys into 4 slices each, coat them with seasoned flour and add them to the pie dish. Cover the meat with a layer of leeks, then a layer of potatoes, and repeat until all the vegetables have been added.

Season well, and pour on the stock. Cover the pie dish with foil and cook on the lowest shelf of a pre-heated oven 180°C/350°F/gas mark 4 for about 1$\frac{1}{2}$ hours. Remove from the oven and allow to cool before rolling out the pastry to make a lid for the pie. Bake in a hotter oven for 30-40 minutes, until golden brown.

The filling for the pie can be cooked the day before it is needed and the pastry lid added the following day.

The pie should be served hot with seasonal vegetables.

Bless us, O Lord, and these your gifts
which we are about to receive, from your bounty
through Christ our Lord. Amen.

Traditional

Our Father in heaven, we give thanks for the
pleasure of gathering together. We give thanks
for life, for freedom to enjoy it all, and all other
blessings. As we partake of this food, we pray for
health and strength to live as you would have us.
Amen.

Harry Jewell

St Clement
23 November

The details of Clement's life are by no means clear, but he is thought to have been the fourth successor to Peter as Pope. He may have known Peter and Paul, and he may be the Clement mentioned in Paul's Letter to the Philippians. He is well known, however, for writing a pastoral letter to the Church in Corinth at a time when there was some disagreement between the Church leaders and their congregation. Clement's letter was the first example of a pope intervening in the affairs of another church, and the letter shows his concern for his flock as well as his advice over their arguments. As a result of his letter, which was well received and frequently read aloud in Corinth, Clement is regarded as the first of the Apostolic Fathers. A number of legends are associated with him: he was said to have been sentenced to hard labour in the Crimea, lashed to an anchor and thrown into the sea. The anchor is Clement's symbol, and the story accounts for numerous connections with fishermen and the sea, such as St Clement's Isle in Mount's Bay, Cornwall, and the Guild of the Holy Trinity and St Clement (now Trinity House) in London. The church of St Clement's Dane in Fleet Street is dedicated to him, and the bells of the church are immortalized in the children's song,

'Oranges and Lemons'. When the River Thames was wider than it is now oranges and lemons were landed at the quay just below St Clement's Dane. An 'oranges and lemons' service is still held at the end of March, when the church is suitably decorated and oranges and lemons are given to the children after the service.

St Clement's feast day is celebrated on 23 November: the bakers of Cambridge used to hold an annual supper known as Bakers' Clem, and in Tenby the fishermen were entertained to a feast of roast goose and rice pudding by the boat-owners. Blacksmiths were once given a 'wayz-goose', a leg of pork stuffed with sage and onions, to celebrate their patron saint. A St Clement's Fair was also held in Sandwich, Kent.

For roast goose, see the recipe in the St Michael's section (p. 134).

Rice pudding

Ingredients

To serve 4 to 6 people

2oz/50g short grain (pudding)
   rice
1 pint/600ml milk
3oz/75g caster sugar
$\frac{1}{2}$ oz/15g butter, cut into
   flakes
$\frac{1}{2}$ tsp grated nutmeg
2 eggs, separated

In the poorer hill-farming regions of Wales, milk sales formed the larger part of the family budget, so milk puddings were a luxury only to be enjoyed on Sundays or 'special' days.

Method

Put the rice in a pan with just enough water to cover it and boil for 5 minutes. Drain if necessary and tip the rice into a buttered 2 pint/1 litre ovenproof dish. Stir in the milk and 2oz/50g of the sugar. Dot with the butter and sprinkle on half the nutmeg.

Bake in a pre-heated oven 170°C/325°F/gas mark 3 for 1 hour. Remove the dish from the oven and allow it to cool for 5 minutes, then beat the egg yolks into the rice. Return the pudding to the oven for a further 30 minutes. During this time beat the egg whites until they are stiff and stir in the remaining 1oz/25g of sugar. Remove the pudding from the oven and allow it to cool for 5 minutes. Now fold in the egg-whites and sprinkle the remaining nutmeg on the top. Return the rice pudding to the oven for a final 15 minutes to set the egg whites.

St Catherine of Alexandria
25 November

Catherine may have existed only as a character in a Greek romance, since no dates are available for her and she is not mentioned in any lists of early martyrs. She was said to be of noble birth, learned and beautiful, and she publicly tested the emperor against the worship of idols, disputing with 50 philosophers. She was able to demolish their arguments and they were put to death. Catherine refused to deny her faith by marrying against her wishes, and she was beaten for two hours before being imprisoned. Here she was fed by a dove and had a vision of Christ.

She was then tied to a spiked wheel (the Catherine wheel) but this broke, and the spikes flew out into the crowd and killed some of them. Her resolution and faith helped to convert 200 soldiers who were then beheaded for their faith. Catherine suffered the same fate. Her feast day is 25 November; it used to be called Cattern Day and was an occasion for partying. People visited each other and were entertained to caraway seed cakes called 'wiggs', and drank elderberry wine or warm beer with beaten eggs and rum in it.

Caraway seed cake can be made using any plain cake recipe with added caraway seeds; in the recipes, one is a lighter version and one, with whisky, is the celebration Scottish version. A wigg recipe is also included as it is different from the seed cakes more usually made today.

Ingredients

3oz/75g butter
6oz/150g caster sugar
3 eggs
8oz/225g self-raising flour
$1/2$oz/15g caraway seeds
A little grated lemon zest

Caraway seed cakes
Method

Cream the butter and sugar together until light and fluffy. Add each egg separately, beating in some flour between each addition of egg to prevent curdling. When all the flour has been mixed in, stir in the caraway seeds and lemon zest. Bake either as a large cake or as individual small cakes in a pre-heated oven 180°C/360°F/gas mark 4 until firm to the touch and golden brown. Cool on a wire rack.

Ingredients

2oz/50g butter
4oz/100g caster sugar
$1/2$ pint/125ml milk
2 egg whites
5oz/125g self-raising flour
1 large tsp caraway seeds

Caraway angel cake
Method

Cream the butter and sugar together until light and fluffy. Stir in the milk slowly and then the egg whites that have been whisked as for meringue. Lightly fold in the flour and the caraway seeds. Bake as a large cake or as small individual cakes in a pre-heated oven 180°C/360°F/gas mark 4 until firm to the touch and light golden brown. Cool on a wire rack.

Scottish seed cake

Ingredients

4oz/100g butter
4oz/100g sugar
6oz/150g self-raising flour
2 eggs
1 tbsp caraway seeds
1 tsp whisky

Scottish seed cake was traditionally eaten on Plough Monday, as well as at other celebrations.

Method

Cream the butter and sugar together until light and fluffy, then mix in the eggs, flour, whisky and caraway seeds. Bake as a large cake or small individual cakes in a pre-heated oven 180°C/350°F/gas mark 4 until firm to the touch and golden brown. Cool on a wire rack.

Wiggs

Ingredients

To make 8 cakes

1lb/450g strong white flour
1 tsp mixed spice
$1/4$oz/7g caraway seeds
2oz/50g sugar
$1/2$oz/15g fresh yeast
1 50mg vitamin C tablet
$1/2$ pint/300ml milk, warmed
2oz/50g butter, melted

These cakes were made for celebrations and other special occasions.

Method

Sift the flour and spice into a mixing bowl and stir in the sugar and caraway seeds. Dissolve the vitamin C tablet in the warm milk and stir in the yeast. Pour this liquid and the melted butter into the flour and knead well.

Turn the dough onto a floured surface and roll it out to 1in/2.5cm thick, then cut out two 6in/15cm rounds. Cut each round into 4 equal triangles and place the cakes onto a greased or lined baking sheet, cover and leave in a warm place to prove for about 30 minutes or until about double in size.

Bake in a pre-heated oven 220°C/425°F/gas mark 7 for 20 minutes or until golden brown. Cool on a wire rack.

Lord of all the pots and pans and things, since I've no time to be a great saint by doing lovely things, or watching late with thee, or dreaming in the dawn light, or storming heaven's gates, make me a saint by getting meals, and washing up the plates.

Warm all the kitchen with thy love, and light it up with thy peace; forgive me all my worrying, and make my grumbling cease.

Thou who didst love to give people food, accept the service that I do – I do it unto thee.

Attributed to St Teresa of Avila

St Andrew
30 November

Andrew and his brother Simon were the first apostles to be called by Jesus. Andrew, a fisherman, lived in the town of Bethsaida, which he left to follow Jesus. He is present on a number of occasions in the gospel stories, but later accounts of his life are unreliable, and details of his ministry uncertain. He may have visited Greece, Syria and Ethiopia, and he was martyred by crucifixion at Patras in Achaia. The idea that he was crucified on an X-shaped cross, the saltire, did not appear until the late Middle Ages. Many claims have been made about his relics, which were taken to a number of places including Italy and Constantinople. According to legend they were also taken to Fife, following which Andrew became the patron saint of Scotland; his cross appears as the emblem on the Scottish flag, and also on the Union Jack.

In Scotland a celebration meal for St Andrew's Day might start with cock-a-leekie soup followed by a main course of haggis, venison, ptarmigan or collops, served with tatties and neeps, and all washed down with whisky. Before the Reformation the men and boys used to go 'Andra-ing' on the morning of St Andrew's Day, to catch rabbits and squirrels for the 'Andrermas' dinner in the evening. Other dishes on the menu for the meal included haggis and singed sheep's head. In England the men and boys were allowed to go squirreling, when they took the opportunity to catch anything that was edible, including hares, pheasants and partridges. Hot elderberry wine was usually drunk with the food or to toast the saint. A selection from this menu would also be suitable for a Burns' Night celebration meal on 25 January.

Cock-a-leekie soup

Ingredients

To serve 4-6 people

1 small boiling fowl or chicken
    with giblets
1 onion, washed and
    quartered but not peeled
2 carrots, washed and
    chopped but not peeled
Bouquet garni
8 peppercorns
1 tsp salt
3 pints/1.7 litres water
1oz/25g butter
6 leeks, trimmed and thinly
    sliced
2 spring onions, trimmed and
    thinly sliced
2 tbsp finely chopped parsley

Whilst this soup is often thought to be Scotland's own dish, it is also made in other parts of the British Isles, especially in Wales and the West Country. The soup used to be made with an old rooster, the tough flesh of which benefits from prolonged simmering. Now good results are obtained using a boiling fowl, roasting chicken or capon. Chunks of chicken and rings of leeks make the soup a meal in itself.

Method

Put the chicken with the giblets in a large saucepan, together with the onion and carrots, bouquet garni, peppercorns and salt and cover with water. Bring to the boil slowly and skim off any fat.

Simmer for $1\frac{1}{4}$ to $1\frac{1}{2}$ hours, until the chicken meat is tender. Remove the chicken from the stock and strain the stock into a bowl.

Chill the stock in the refrigerator until the fatty layer has hardened and can be removed. Discard the carrots, onions and giblets. Once the chicken has cooled cut the flesh into chunky pieces, discarding the skin and bones.

Put the butter into a large saucepan and heat gently, add the leeks and spring onions and cook for about 15 minutes, until they are soft and transparent. Add the stock and heat for a further 15 minutes. Season with salt and pepper. Add the chunks of chicken and heat for a further 10 minutes, stir in the chopped parsley and serve.

Venison stew

Ingredients

2lb/900g venison meat from the haunch or shoulder
Seasoned flour
1oz/25g butter
2 tbsp cooking oil
1 pint/575ml red wine or stock or a mixture of the two
$\frac{1}{4}$ tsp grated nutmeg
1 blade of mace
4 whole cloves
1 stick of cinnamon
$\frac{1}{4}$ tsp cayenne pepper

Method

Cut the venison into 1in/2.5cm cubes and coat them in the seasoned flour. Heat the butter and oil in a frying pan and quickly brown the cubes of meat.

Put the venison into a casserole with a well-fitting lid. Pour the wine/stock into the frying pan and stir to mix in the venison juices left in the pan. Now pour the stock into the casserole and add the spices and season with salt. Cover the casserole and put it into a pre-heated oven 180°C/350°F/gas mark 4. Cook gently for $1\frac{1}{2}$-2 hours or until the meat is tender. Remove the cinnamon stick before serving.

Creamed potatoes, braised celery and green vegetables go well with this dish.

Haggis

Haggis is really a large mutton sausage, originally made by sheep farmers as a way to use the heart, liver and lights of the sheep. Haggis can be made at home but it is readily available in supermarkets, delicatessens and butchers' shops. Vegetarian haggis is also available.

Ptarmigan

Fresh game birds need to be hung for 3-4 days to allow the flavour to develop. If a frozen bird is used it must be completely thawed before cooking.

Method

Allow one bird per person. If the ptarmigan are to be stuffed, put the mixture in the neck-end cavity. If you are not using stuffing, a peeled onion, a peeled and cored apple, or butter flavoured with lemon rind or herbs can be put in the body cavity to add flavour.

Truss the bird neatly so that it keeps a good shape. As the meat can be dry, spread butter over the breast and then cover with streaky bacon rashers. Pre-heat the oven to 190°C/375°F/gas mark 5. Allow 35-40 minutes for a ptarmigan to cook and baste it frequently with butter during this time.

If the breast seems to be browning too quickly cover it with foil. For a golden brown, crispy finish to the birds, remove the bacon rashers 10 minutes before the end of the cooking time, baste the breast well with butter and pan juices, dredge with seasoned flour, baste again and return to the oven.

Ptarmigan is best served with bread sauce, fried breadcrumbs, hot game chips and redcurrant or rowan jelly.

Collops are eaten on St Andrew's Day. For the recipe see p. 31.

St Lucy
13 December

Lucy is thought to have lived in Syracuse, and died there in the persecutions of Emperor Diocletian around AD303-5. Various stories surround her martyrdom: she refused to marry, suffered attempted violation, and was taken to a brothel; but it is probably correct that she died, from a sword thrust, for her faith, and was venerated by the Church as a virgin martyr. Her name is associated with light and purity; she was once invoked against eye disease and is represented in art holding two eyes in a dish.

Lucia buns

Ingredients

To make 12 buns

12oz/350g strong white flour
$1/4$ pint/150ml warm milk
1oz/25g fresh yeast
2oz/50g sugar
3oz/75g melted butter
$1/2$ tsp salt
A pinch of saffron

For the decoration

$1/2$ tsp ground cardamon
4oz/100g seedless raisins
A little beaten egg
2oz/50g cube sugar

These buns were made by the daughters of the family for their friends and relations on St Lucy's Day, and also to mark the beginning of the Christmas celebrations. In some European countries St Lucy's Day is widely celebrated with special meals and traditions.

Method

Sift the flour into a mixing bowl. Mix the yeast with a teaspoon of sugar in half the milk. Mix the melted butter with the rest of the milk and the sugar, salt and saffron, then add this to the yeast mixture.

Pour this mixture into the flour and work into a soft dough, kneading lightly. Cover and leave in a warm place to rise for 1 hour.

Now divide the dough into 24 equal pieces and roll each into a length of about 12in/30cms. Coil the ends in opposite directions to make an 'S' shape with a long body.

Take two of these 'S's and join them together in a cross shape, putting a pinch of cardamon and some raisins where the two 'S's meet and in the centre of the coils.

Place the buns on greased or lined baking sheets, cover and leave them to prove for a further 20 minutes.

Before putting them in the oven, brush the tops with a little beaten egg and sprinkle with crushed sugar cubes. Bake in a pre-heated oven 220°C/425°F/gas mark 7 for 20 minutes. Cool on a wire rack.

Sources

For Information

Introduction to Christian Worship (revised edition) by James F. White, Abingdon Press 1992 ISBN 0 687 19508 X

The Oxford Book of Saints by David Hugh Farmer, OUP ISBN 0 1986 094 93

The Penguin Dictionary of Saints by Donald Attwater with Catherine Rachael John, Penguin Books 1995 ISBN 0 14 051312 4

AA Places to Visit in Britain, Drive Publications 1988

AA Book of British Villages, Drive Publications 1980

British Folk Customs by Christine Hole

Also pamphlets etc. received from:
> Fife Council Museums West
> The Mevagissey and District Museum Society
> St Ives Town Council
> Holsworthy Museum
> Museum Resource Centre, Colchester Borough Council
> Margate Old Town Hall Local History Museum
> Cultural and Leisure Services, Glasgow Borough Council
> Sandwich Guildhall Museum
> The Corporation of Trinity House
> Winchester Museum Services, Winchester City Council
> Inverkeithing Local History Society
> Barnstaple Town Guide
> Warrington Borough Council, Museums Department

For Information and Recipes Ideas

Readers Digest Farmhouse Cookery by various authors, The Readers Digest Association Ltd 1980 ISBN 0 276 42086 1

Feasting and Festivals by Jan Wilson, Sandy Lane Books 1990 ISBN 0 7459 4006 4

The London Ritz Book of Afternoon Tea by Helen Simpson, Edbury Press 1986 ISBN 0 85223 422 8

East Anglian Recipes – 300 years of housewife's choice by Mary Norwak, East Anglian Magazine Ltd 1978 ISBN 0 9002277 30 3

English Heritage Series – Food and Cooking, History and Recipes:
>   18th Century Britain by Jennifer Stead 1985 ISBN 1 85074 538 2
>   17th Century Britain by Peter Brears 1985 ISBN 1 85074 537 4
>   16th Century Britain by Peter Brears 1985 ISBN 1 85074 536 6
>   Medieval Britain by Maggie Black 1985 ISBN 1 85074 535 8

For Recipe Ideas

The Dairy Book of British Food, Edbury Press 1988 ISBN 0 85223 735 9

The Cooking Canon by Revd John Eley, BBC 1984 ISBN 0 563 20259 9

Lakeland Cookery collected by Cumbria Dalesman Books 1976 ISBN 85206 069 6

Dorset Dishes by Kate Easlea, Paul Cave Publications 1979

West Country Larder compiled by Alison Ainsworth, Penninsula Press 1990 ISBN 1 872640 04 4

West Country Recipes by Rowena Trevelyon, Price Publications 1979

Vegetarian Kitchen by Sarah Brown, BBC 1984 ISBN 0 563 210346 6

Farmhouse Fare compiled by Farmers Weekly Readers, Longacre Press 1954

Granny's Cookery Book by Frances Kitchen, David and Charles 1978 ISBN 0 7153 7721 3

Favourite Recipes Series published by Salmon, English Recipes ISBN 1 89 8435 64 2

Devonshire Recipes compiled by Amanda Persey ISBN 0 90619896 8

Farmhouse Recipes by Carole Gregory ISBN 0 90619891 7

Irish Recipes ISBN 1 8984355 63 4

Kentish Recipes compiled by Pat Smith ISBN 1 898435 05 7

Suffolk Recipes compiled by Dorothy Baldock ISBN 1 898435 09 X

The W.I. Books of Recipes, W.I. Books:
>   *Biscuits* 1984 ISBN 0 900 985 ISBN 0 900 556 85 4
>   *Cakes* by Lyn Mann 1985 ISBN 0 900 556 96 X
>   *Bread and Buns* by Mary Norwak 1984 ISBN 0 900 556 82 X
>   *Puddings* by Janet Wier 1984 ISBN 0 900 556 84 6

Good Food Magazine 1994

Recipes in alphabetical order

Services combining a meal with prayer on Maundy Thursday